W9-BYZ-281

SMART AND GETS THINGS DONE

Joel Spolsky's Concise Guide to Finding the Best Technical Talent

Joel Spolsky

Apress®

Smart and Gets Things Done: Joel Spolsky's Concise Guide to
Finding the Best Technical Talent

Copyright © 2007 by Joel Spolsky

ISBN-13: 978-1-59059-838-2

ISBN-10: 1-59059-838-5

Printed and bound in the United States of America 9 8 7 6 5 4 3 2 1

Lead Editor: Gary Cornell
Editorial Board: Steve Anglin, Ewan Buckingham, Gary Cornell,
    Jason Gilmore, Jonathan Gennick, Jonathan Hassell, Chris Mills,
    Matthew Moodie, Jeffrey Pepper, Dominic Shakeshaft, Matt Wade
Project Manager: Kylie Johnston
Copy Edit Manager: Nicole Flores
Copy Editor: Ami Knox
Assistant Production Director: Kari Brooks-Copony
Production Editor: Laura Cheu
Compositor: Dina Quan
Proofreader: Lori Bring
Indexer: Carol Burbo
Artist: April Milne
Interior and Cover Illustrations: Terry Colon
Cover Designer: Kurt Krames
Manufacturing Director: Tom Debolski

Distributed to the book trade worldwide by Springer-Verlag
New York, Inc., 233 Spring Street, 6th Floor, New York, NY
10013. Phone 1-800-SPRINGER, fax 201-348-4505, e-mail
orders-ny@springer-sbm.com, or visit http://www.
springeronline.com.

For information on translations, please contact Apress directly at
2855 Telegraph Avenue, Suite 600, Berkeley, CA 94705. Phone
510-549-5930, fax 510-549-5939, e-mail info@apress.com, or
visit http://www.apress.com.

For Jared

CONTENTS

ABOUT THE AUTHOR

Joel Spolsky is a globally recognized expert on the software development process. His website, *Joel on Software* (www.joelonsoftware.com), is popular with software developers around the world and has been translated into over 30 languages. As the founder of Fog Creek Software in New York City, he created FogBugz, a popular project management system for software teams. Joel has worked at Microsoft, where, as a member of the Excel team, he designed VBA, and at Juno Online Services, developing an Internet client used by millions. He has written two previous books: *User Interface Design for Programmers* (Apress, 2001) and *Joel on Software* (Apress, 2004), and is the editor of *The Best Software Writing I* (Apress, 2005). Joel holds a BS from Yale in computer science. He served in the Israeli Defense Forces as a paratrooper, and was one of the founders of Kibbutz Hanaton.

INTRODUCTION

Imagine, if you will, a course with ten obstacles.

A bunch of runners stand at the beginning. There's a two-story wall you have to jump over, there's some kind of rope bridge, snakes on a plane, whatever.

For simplicity, assume that each obstacle successfully stops 50% of the runners.

So if twelve runners start out, after the very first obstacle, six of them will somehow find themselves defeated. You will see them piled in a heap at the bottom of the two-story wall.

The remaining six will move on to the rope bridge, where three will fall through the ropes in a humorous way, eventually finding themselves dangling by one foot in the air, with all kinds of silly things falling out of their pockets. Keys, wallets, coins, yes, but also rubber duckies, kazoos, sliding trombones. You know. Silly things.

Nobody, really, will make it past all ten obstacles.

In fact, if you want to get just one person to pass all ten, you are going to have to start out with 2^{10} runners on the start line. That's 1,024 runners.

The process of hiring great technical talent is an elimination course. A lot of people have never heard of your company. A lot of the people who are left don't know that you're hiring. Others live in the wrong city. Still others don't have the right visas. Others send in the resume but John, who reads them all, tends to throw away the resumes from schools who beat him when he was on the football team at Columbia. Still others came in for the interview and bombed. Of the remainder, some were pretty good but had other job offers. Those who didn't have other job offers were so distressed by the peeling, gray paint on the walls and the nasty fluorescent lighting that they stayed at their current job. And a few who didn't mind the cubicles decided that they really didn't want to program bunker-buster bombs for a living. Not that there's anything wrong with bunker-buster bombs; it just wasn't for them. Weenies.

This obstacle-course reality of hiring sounds depressing. It really does. Does it mean we have to start with 3,000 candidates to hire three programmers?

But there's a silver lining, if you will: a bright side to all this meandering mathematical moroseness. And that is this: if you can eliminate *one* obstacle—just one!—you can *double* the number of people you hire. Eliminate two obstacles, and you quadruple the number that make it past the remaining obstacles. And so on, and so forth.

But there is no silver bullet. There is no magical single thing you can do to solve all your hiring problems and get great developers working for you tomorrow. What you have to do is look at the whole process as an obstacle course and start to think about how to eliminate as many obstacles as possible. Work on all of them, because they're all equally important.

If your title is "technical recruiter" or something in Human Resources, you might notice a small problem beginning to emerge. In fact, if your title is anything other than "Lord High Supreme Ruler, Commander of the Empire and Queen of All Bees," you might have this problem: sometimes the obstacles to recruiting are not your fault and they're not under your control. If people don't want to work for your company because they'd be working in a loud, dark, windowless room with cubicles, flickering lighting, old ratty carpets, and a distinct smell of mildew, well, that's a facilities problem, not a recruiting problem, right? Sorry, I know it's not your *fault*, but it *is* your problem. A lot of the things I'm going to be talking about that you need to do to recruit great developers are outside of the scope of the normal recruiter. Heck, many of them are things that even the CEO can't control.

All is not lost. You should at least have an awareness of what these issues are, so you know what to lobby for. If you're having trouble recruiting because the office space is awful, well, even though it's not traditionally a recruiter's job, you're going to have to inject yourself forcefully into the next office planning session. If the company is located in a place that doesn't attract bright college graduates, that's something to talk to your CEO about the next time he yells at you for not filling those openings. In the meantime, you can work on the other parts of the obstacle course that *are* under your control, and you should still see positive results.

The Story Behind This Book

A long time ago, in the year 2000 to be exact, I wrote an embarrassing article on my website called "Whaddaya mean, you can't find pro-grammers?"[1]

Way back then, the first dotcom boom was well underway, and the demand for web pro-grammers was so high that a lot of big companies had taken to bringing in IT consult-ing firms and paying $200 or $300 an hour for not-very-good HTML coders. A new corps of Internet consultants sprung up, hiring 22-year old college grads who knew how to use FrontPage. They earned about $40 an hour, but could be billed out at $250 an hour.

The article purported to explain that if you just pay enough, offer well-lit offices, and gave people massages, you shouldn't have any prob-lem hiring.

Shortly after I wrote that article, though, the first Internet bubble burst, and we had some-thing of a nuclear winter in the tech industry. Tons of programmers, developers, web designers, and producers were dumped unceremoniously on the street, many of whom didn't realize that $60,000 was not really a realistic starting salary for college graduates who had majored in

---

1. Normally I would put the URL here so you could look it up. But that old article I wrote in my youth is just ridic-ulous, so, while it's still on the Web, you'll have to find it for yourself, which I don't recommend.

English and whose only technical skills involved creating their own personal homepage on Geocities. Programmers were happy to take any job they could find, even working at (*hold nose*) the dreaded Microsoft (*shudder*). For the next three or four years, I was totally embarrassed to have written something so callous when so many talented (and untalented) programmers were moving back in with their parents and taking jobs at Staples.

When I looked back on that article recently, I realized something: I had written it without really completely knowing what I was talking about. I had a few ideas about how to hire programmers, but I didn't really have any real-world experience.

Over the last six years, my friend Michael and I have been building a software company. From the very beginning, we were always *totally* convinced that our *number one* priority was hiring great people, even before we knew what kind of software we would make. Over those years, we focused incessantly on getting great people to want to work for us—even before we could afford to hire anyone. We made some mistakes, and we learned a lot, but now I feel like getting good people to work at Fog Creek is practically the only problem we *don't* have. I know so much more about the whole process of recruiting great talent than I did when I wrote the original article that I cringe when I look back on it.

And something else changed in the last year or so: the winter ended. Tech investment is back. New startups are appearing left and right, and most of the more established technology companies are once again hiring like crazy. Just about every company that hires software developers has a long list of openings. The ones that don't are, for the most part, smart, boot-strapped startups that are trying to live off of the money that they actually earn by selling things to customers, a much healthier situation than we had in 2000. On the whole, the openings I see out there now are for companies that have plenty of money and plenty of customers, and they're hiring because they just want to reinvest profits and grow. What I'm *not* seeing is a job market dominated by a lot of crazy VC-funded startups who naturally assume that 170 employees are about the right amount for a new company, so the first thing they do is hire 170 people.

And once again, managers, entrepreneurs, and recruiting directors, already long-since completely convinced that hiring great software developers is critical, have begun to wonder just why it's so hard to fill all those openings they have. So, in the hopes that it will in some way atone for my first embarrassing effort, I've written this book.

And I hope it will help you make your organization a great place to work, and by doing so, increase, in some small way, the amount of happiness in the world.

Chapter 1

HITTING THE HIGH NOTES

In March 2000, I launched the website *Joel on Software*[1] by making the very shaky claim that most people are wrong in thinking you need an idea to make a successful software company:

> *The common belief is that when you're building a software company, the goal is to find a neat idea that solves some problem which hasn't been solved before, implement it, and make a fortune. We'll call this the build-a-better-mousetrap belief. But the real goal for software companies should be converting capital into software that works.*[2]

---

1. www.joelonsoftware.com

2. Joel Spolsky, "Converting Capital Into Software That Works," published at www.joelonsoftware.com on March 21, 2000 (search for "Converting Capital").

For the last five years, I've been testing that theory in the real world. The formula for Fog Creek Software, the company I started with Michael Pryor in September 2000, can be summarized in four steps:

It's a pretty convenient formula, especially since our *real* goal in starting Fog Creek was to create a software company where *we would want to work*. I made the claim, in those days, that good working conditions (or, awkwardly, "building the company where the best software developers in the world would want to work") would *lead* to profits as naturally as chocolate leads to chubbiness, and cartoon sex in video games leads to gangland-style shooting sprees.

For today, though, I want to answer just one question, because if this part isn't true, the whole theory falls apart. That question is, does it even make sense to talk about having the "best programmers"? Is there so much variation between programmers that this even matters?

Maybe it's obvious to us, but to many, the assertion still needs to be proven.

Several years ago a larger company was considering buying out Fog Creek, and I knew it would never work as soon as I heard the CEO of that company say that he didn't really agree with my theory of hiring the best programmers. He used a biblical metaphor: you only need one King David, and an army of soldiers who merely had to be able to carry out orders. His company's stock price promptly dropped from $20 to $5, so it's a good thing we didn't take the offer, but it's hard to pin that on the King David fetish.

And in fact, the conventional wisdom in the world of copycat business journalists and large companies who rely on overpaid management consultants to think for them, chew their food, etc., seems to be that the most important thing is reducing the *cost* of programmers.

In some other industries, cheap *is* more important than good. Wal-Mart grew to be the biggest corporation on Earth by selling cheap products, not good products. If Wal-Mart tried to sell high-quality goods, their costs would go up, and their whole cheap advantage would be lost. For example, if they tried to sell a tube sock that can withstand the unusual rigors of, say, being washed in a washing machine, they'd have to use all kinds of expensive components, like, say, *cotton,* and the cost for every single sock would go up.

So, why isn't there room in the software industry for a low-cost provider, someone who uses the cheapest programmers available? (Remind me to ask Quark how that whole fire-everybody-and-hire-low-cost-replacements plan is working.)

Here's why: duplication of software is free. That means the cost of programmers is spread out over all the copies of the software you sell. With software, you can improve quality without adding to the incremental cost of each unit sold.

Essentially, *design adds value faster than it adds cost.*

Or, roughly speaking, if you try to skimp on programmers, you'll make crappy software, and you won't even save that much money.

The same thing applies to the entertainment industry. It's worth hiring Brad Pitt for your latest blockbuster movie, even though he demands a high salary, because that salary can be divided by all the millions of people who see the movie solely because Brad is so damn *hot*.

Or, to put it another way, it's worth hiring Angelina Jolie for your latest blockbuster movie, even though she demands a high salary, because that salary can be divided by all the millions of people who see the movie solely because Angelina is so damn *hot*.

But I still haven't proven anything. What does it mean to be "the best programmer," and are there really such major variations between the quality of software produced by different programmers?

Let's start with plain old productivity. It's rather hard to measure programmer productivity; almost any metric you can come up with (lines of debugged code, function points, number of command-line arguments) is trivial to game, and it's very hard to get concrete data on large projects because it's very rare for two programmers to be told to do the same thing.

The data I rely upon comes from Professor Stanley Eisenstat at Yale. Each year he teaches a programming-intensive course, CS 323, where a large proportion of the work consists of about five programming assignments, each of which takes about two weeks. The assignments are very serious for a college class: implement a Unix command-line shell, implement a ZLW file compressor, etc.

There was so much griping among the students about how much work was required for this class that Professor Eisenstat started asking the students to report back on how much time they spent on each assignment. He has collected this data carefully for several years.

I spent some time crunching his numbers; it's the only data set I know of that measures dozens of students working on identical assignments using the same technology at the same time. It's pretty darn controlled, as experiments go.

The first thing I did with this data was to calculate the average, minimum, maximum, and standard deviation of hours spent on each of the twelve assignments. The results:

Project	Avg hours	Min hours	Max hours	StDev hours
CMDLINE99	14.84	4.67	29.25	5.82
COMPRESS00	33.83	11.58	77.00	14.51
COMPRESS01	25.78	10.00	48.00	9.96
COMPRESS99	27.47	6.67	69.50	13.62
LEXHIST01	17.39	5.50	39.25	7.39
MAKE01	22.03	8.25	51.50	8.91
MAKE99	22.12	6.77	52.75	10.72
SHELL00	22.98	10.00	38.68	7.17
SHELL01	17.95	6.00	45.00	7.66
SHELL99	20.38	4.50	41.77	7.03
TAR00	12.39	4.00	69.00	10.57
TEX00	21.22	6.00	75.00	12.11
ALL PROJECTS	**21.44**	**4.00**	**77.00**	**11.16**

The most obvious thing you notice here is the huge variations. The fastest students were finishing three or four times faster than the average students and as much as ten times faster than the slowest students. The standard deviation is outrageous. So then I thought, hmm, maybe some of these students are doing a terrible job. I didn't want to include students who spent four hours on the assignment without producing a working program. So I narrowed the data down and only included the data from students who were in the top quartile of grades... the top 25% in terms of the quality of the code. I should mention that grades in Professor Eisenstat's class are *completely* objective: they're calculated formulaically based on how many automated tests the code passes and nothing else. No points are deducted for bad style.

Anyway, here are the results for the top quartile:

Project	Avg hours	Min hours	Max hours	StDev hours
CMDLINE99	13.89	8.68	29.25	6.55
COMPRESS00	37.40	23.25	77.00	16.14
COMPRESS01	23.76	15.00	48.00	11.14
COMPRESS99	20.95	6.67	39.17	9.70
LEXHIST01	14.32	7.75	22.00	4.39
MAKE01	22.02	14.50	36.00	6.87
MAKE99	22.54	8.00	50.75	14.80

Continued

Project	Avg hours	Min hours	Max hours	StDev hours
SHELL00	23.13	18.00	30.50	4.27
SHELL01	16.20	6.00	34.00	8.67
SHELL99	20.98	13.15	32.00	5.77
TAR00	11.96	6.35	18.00	4.09
TEX00	16.58	6.92	30.50	7.32
ALL PROJECTS	20.49	6.00	77.00	10.93

Not much difference! The standard deviation is almost exactly the same for the top quartile. In fact, when you look closely at the data, it's pretty clear there's *no discernable correlation between the time and score.* Here's a typical scatter plot of one of the assignments... I chose the assignment COMPRESS01, an implementation of Ziv-Lempel-Welch compression assigned to students in 2001, because the standard deviation there is close to the overall standard deviation.

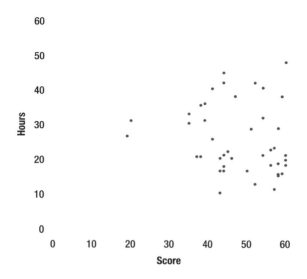

There's just nothing to see here, and that's the point. *The quality of the work and the amount of time spent are simply uncorrelated.*

I asked Professor Eisenstat about this, and he pointed out one more thing: because assignments are due at a fixed time (usually midnight) and the penalties for being late are significant, a lot of students stop before the project is done. In other words, the maximum time spent on these assignments is as low as it is partially because there just aren't enough hours between the time the assignment is handed out and the time it is due. If students had unlimited time to work on the projects (which would correspond a little better to the working world), the spread could only be *higher*.

This data is not completely scientific. There's probably some cheating. Some students may exaggerate the time spent on assignments in hopes of gaining some sympathy and getting easier assignments the next time. (Good luck! The assignments in CS 323 are the same today as they were when I took the class in the 1980s.) Other students may underreport because they lost track of time. Still, I don't think it's a stretch to believe this data shows 5 to 1 or 10 to 1 productivity differences between programmers.

But Wait, There's More!

If the only difference between programmers were productivity, you might think that you could substitute five mediocre programmers for one really good programmer. That obviously doesn't work. Brooks' Law, "Adding manpower to a late software project makes it later," is why.[3] A single good programmer working on a single task has no coordination or communication overhead. Five programmers working on

---

3. Frederick Brooks, *The Mythical Man-Month: Essays on Software Engineering* (Reading, Mass.: Addison-Wesley, 1975).

the same task must coordinate and communicate. That takes a lot of time. There are added benefits to using the smallest team possible; the man-month really is mythical.

But Wait, There's Even More!

The real trouble with using a lot of mediocre programmers instead of a couple of good ones is that no matter how long they work, they never produce something as good as what the great programmers can produce.

Five Antonio Salieris won't produce Mozart's *Requiem*. Ever. Not if they work for 100 years.

Five Jim Davises—creator of that unfunny cartoon cat, where 20% of the jokes are about how Monday sucks and the rest are about how much the cat likes lasagna (and those are the *punchlines!*)—five Jim Davises could spend the rest of their *lives* writing comedy and never, ever produce the "Soup Nazi" episode of *Seinfeld*.

The Creative Zen team could spend years refining their ugly iPod knockoffs and never produce as beautiful, satisfying, and elegant a player as the Apple iPod. And they're not going to make a dent in Apple's market share because the magical design talent is just *not there*. They *don't have it*.

The mediocre talent just *never hits the high notes* that the top talent hits all the time. The number of divas who can hit the F6 in Mozart's "Queen of the Night" is vanishingly small, and you just can't perform "Queen of the Night" without that famous F6.

Is software really about artistic high notes? "Maybe some stuff is," you say, "but I work on accounts receivable user interfaces for the medical waste industry." Fair enough. My focus is on product companies, where success or failure depends on the quality of the product. If you're only using software internally to support your operations, you probably only need software to be good enough.

And we've seen plenty of examples of great software, the really high notes, in the past few years: stuff that mediocre software developers just *could not* have developed.

Back in 2003, Nullsoft shipped a new version of Winamp, with the following notice on their website:

- Snazzy new look!
- Groovy new features!
- Most things actually work!

It's the last part—the "Most things actually work!"—that makes everyone laugh. And then they're happy, and so they get excited about Winamp, and they use it, and tell their friends, and they think Winamp is awesome, all because they actually wrote on their website, "Most things actually work!" How cool is that?

If you threw a bunch of extra programmers onto the Windows Media Player team, would they ever hit that high note? Never in a thousand years. Because the more people you added to that team, the more likely they would be to have one real grump who thought it was unprofessional and immature to write "Most things actually work" on your website.

Not to mention the comment, "Winamp 3: Almost as new as Winamp 2!"

That kind of stuff is what made us love Winamp.

By the time AOL Time Warner Corporate Weenieheads got their hands on that thing, the funny stuff from the website was gone. You can just see them, fuming and festering and sniveling like Salieri in the movie *Amadeus*, trying to beat down all signs of creativity that might scare one old lady in Minnesota, at the cost of wiping out anything that might have made people *like* the product.

Or look at the iPod. *You can't change the battery*. So when the battery dies, *too bad. Get a new iPod*. Actually, Apple will replace it if you send it back to the factory, but that costs $65.95. Wowza.

Why can't you change the battery?

My theory is that it's because Apple didn't want to mar the otherwise perfectly smooth, seamless surface of their beautiful, sexy iPod with one of those ghastly battery covers you see on other cheapo consumer crap, with the little latches that are always breaking and the seams that fill up with pocket lint and all that general yuckiness. The iPod is the most seamless piece of consumer electronics I have ever seen. It's beautiful. It *feels* beautiful, like a smooth river stone. One battery latch can blow the whole river stone effect.

Apple made a decision based on *style*; in fact, iPod is full of decisions that are based on style. And style is not something that 100 programmers at Microsoft or 200 industrial designers at the inaptly named Creative are going to be able to achieve, because they don't have Jonathan Ive, and there aren't a heck of a lot of Jonathan Ives floating around.

I'm sorry, I can't stop talking about the iPod. That beautiful thumbwheel with its little clicky sounds... Apple spent *extra money* putting a speaker *in the iPod itself* so that the thumb-wheel clicky sounds would come from the thumbwheel. They could have saved pennies—*pennies!*—by playing the clicky sounds through the headphones. But the thumbwheel makes you feel like you're in control. People like to feel in control. *It makes people happy to feel in control.* The fact that the thumbwheel responds smoothly, fluently, and *audibly* to your commands makes you *happy*. Not like the other 6,000 pocket-sized consumer electronics bits of junk which take so long booting up that when you hit the on/off switch you have to wait a minute to find out if anything happened. Are you in control? Who knows? When was the last time you had a cell phone that went on the instant you pressed the on button?

Style.

Happiness.

Emotional appeal.

These are what make the huge hits, in software products, in movies, and in consumer electronics. And if you don't get this stuff right, you may solve the problem, but your product doesn't become the #1 hit that makes everybody in the company rich so you can *all* drive stylish, happy, appealing cars like the Ferrari Spider F1 and still have enough money left over to build an ashram in your backyard.

It's not just a matter of "10 times more productive." It's that the "average productive" developer never hits the high notes that make great software.

Sadly, this doesn't really apply in nonproduct software development. Internal, in-house software is rarely important enough to justify hiring rock stars. Nobody hires Dolly Parton to sing at weddings. That's why the most satisfying careers, if you're a software developer, are at actual software companies, not doing IT for some bank.

The software marketplace, these days, is something of a winner-take-all system. Nobody else is making money on MP3 players other than Apple. Nobody else makes money on spreadsheets and word processors other than Microsoft, and, yes, I know, they did anticompetitive things to get into that position, but that doesn't change the fact that it's a winner-take-all system.

You can't afford to be number two, or to have a "good enough" product. It has to be remarkably good, by which I mean so good that people remark about it. The lagniappe that you get from the really, really, really talented software developers is your only hope for remarkableness. It's all in the plan:

Chapter 2

FINDING GREAT DEVELOPERS

Where Are All Those Great Developers?

The first time you try to fill an open position, if you're like most people, you place some ads, maybe browse around the large online boards, and get a ton of resumes.

As you go through them, you think, "Hmm, this might work," or, "No way!" or, "I wonder if this person could be convinced to move to Buffalo." What *doesn't* happen, and I guarantee this, what *never* happens is that you say, "Wow, this person is brilliant! We must have them!" In fact, you can go through thousands of resumes, assuming you know how to read resumes, which is not easy, and I'll get to that in Chapter 4, but you can go through thousands of job applications and quite frankly never see a great software developer. Not a one.

Here is why this happens.

The great software developers, indeed, the best people in every field, are quite simply *never on the market*.

The average great software developer will apply for, total, *maybe,* four jobs in their entire career.

The great college graduates get pulled into an internship by a professor with a connection to industry, then they get early offers from that company and never bother applying for any other jobs. If they leave that company, it's often to go to a startup with a friend, or to follow a great boss to another company, or because they decided they really want to work on, say, Eclipse, because Eclipse is cool, so they look for an Eclipse job at BEA or IBM and then of course they get it because they're brilliant.

If you're *lucky*, if you're *really lucky*, they show up on the open job market once, when, say, their spouse decides to accept a medical internship in Anchorage and they actually send their resume out to what they think are the few places they'd like to work at in Anchorage.

But for the most part, great developers (and this is almost a tautology) are, uh, great, (OK, it is a tautology), and, usually, prospective employers recognize their greatness quickly, which means, basically, they get to work wherever they want, so they honestly don't send out a lot of resumes or apply for a lot of jobs.

Does this sound like the kind of person you want to hire? It should.

The corollary of that rule—the rule that the great people are never on the market—is that the bad people—the seriously unqualified—are on the market *quite a lot*. They get fired all the time, because they can't do their job. Their companies fail—sometimes because any company that would hire them would probably also hire a lot of unqualified programmers, so it all adds up to failure—but sometimes because they *actually are so unqualified that they ruined the company.* Yep, it happens.

These morbidly unqualified people rarely get jobs, thankfully, but they do keep applying, and when they apply, they go to Monster.com and check off 300 or 1000 jobs at once trying to win the lottery.

Numerically, great people are pretty rare, and they're never on the job market, while incompetent people, even though they are *just as rare*, apply to thousands of jobs throughout their career. So now, Sparky, back to that big pile of resumes you got off of Craigslist. Is it any surprise that most of them are people you don't want to hire?

Astute readers, I expect, will point out that I'm leaving out the largest group yet: the solid, competent people. They're on the market more than the great people, but less than the incompetent, and all in all they will show up in *small* numbers in your 1000 resume pile, but for the most part, almost every hiring manager in Palo Alto right now with 1000 resumes on their desk has the same exact set of 970 resumes from the same minority of 970 incompetent people that are applying for every job in Palo Alto, and probably will be for life, and only 30 resumes even worth considering, of which maybe, rarely, one is a great programmer. OK, maybe not even one. And figuring out how to find those needles in a haystack, we shall see, is possible but not easy.

Can I Get Them Anyway?

Yes!

Well, Maybe!

Or perhaps, It Depends!

Instead of thinking as recruiting as a "gather resumes, filter resumes" procedure, you're going to have to think of it as a "track down the winners and make them talk to you" procedure.

I have three basic methods for how to go about this:

1.   Go to the mountain

2.   Internships

3.   Build your own community*

"Build your own community" comes with a little asterisk that means "hard," like the famous math problem that George Dantzig solved because he came into class too late to hear that it was supposed to be unsolvable.[1]

You can probably come up with your own ideas, too. I'm just going to talk about three that worked for me.

To the Mountain, Jeeves!

Think about where the people you want to hire are hanging out. What conferences do they go to? Where do they live? What organizations do they belong to? What websites do they read?

---

1.   Donald J. Albers and Constance Reid, "An Interview of George B. Dantzig: The Father of Linear Programming," *College Mathematics Journal* 17, no. 4 (1986), pp. 293–314.

Instead of casting a wide net with a job search on Monster.com, use the *Joel on Software* job board (jobs.joelonsoftware.com) and limit your search to the smart developers who read my website. Go to the really interesting tech conferences. Great Mac developers will be at Apple's WWDC. Great Windows programmers will be at Microsoft's PDC. There are a bunch of open source conferences, too.

Look for the hot new technology of the day. Last year it was Python; this year it's Ruby. Go to their conferences where you'll find early adopters who are curious about new things and always interested in improving.

Slink around in the hallways, talk to everyone you meet, go to the technical sessions and invite the speakers out for a beer, and when you find someone smart, BANG!—you launch into full-fledged flirt and flattery mode. "Ooooh, that's so *interesting!*" you say. "Wow, I can't believe you're so *smart*. And handsome, too. Where did you say you work? Really? *There?* Hmmmmmmm. Don't you think you could do better? I think my company might be hiring…"

The corollary of this rule is to *avoid* advertising on general-purpose, large job boards. One summer, I inadvertently advertised our summer internships using MonsterTRAK, which offered the option to pay a little extra to make the internship visible to students at every school in the USA. This resulted in literally hundreds of resumes, not one of which made it past the first round. We ended up spending a ton of money to get a ton of resumes that stood almost no chance at finding the kind of people we wanted to hire. After a few days of this, the very fact that MonsterTRAK was the source of a resume made me think that the candidate was probably not for us. Similarly, when Craigslist first started up and was really just visited by early adopters in the Internet industry, we found great people by advertising on Craigslist, but today, virtually everyone who is moderately computer literate uses it, resulting in too many resumes with too low of a needle-to-haystack ratio.

Internships

One good way to snag the great people who are never on the job market is to get them before they even realize there *is* a job market: when they're in college.

Some hiring managers hate the idea of hiring interns. They see interns as unformed and insufficiently skilled. To some extent, that's true. Interns are not as experienced as experienced employees (no, really?!). You're going to have to invest in them a little bit more, and it's going to take some time before they're up to speed. The good news about our field is that the really great programmers often started programming when they were ten years old. And while everyone else their age was running around playing "soccer" (this is a game many kids who can't program computers play that involves kicking a spherical object called a "ball" with their feet (I know, it sounds weird)), they were in their dad's home office trying to get the Linux kernel to compile. Instead of chasing girls in the playground, they were getting into flamewars on Usenet about the utter depravity of programming languages that don't implement Haskell-style type inference. Instead of starting a band in their garage, they were implementing a cool hack so that when their neighbor stole bandwidth over their open-access Wi-Fi point, all the images on the web appeared upside-down. BWA HA HA HA HA!

So, unlike, say, the fields of law or medicine, over here in software development, by the time these kids are in their second or third year in college, they are pretty darn good programmers.

Pretty much everyone applies for *one* job: their first one, and most kids think that it's OK to wait until their last year to worry about this.

And in fact, most kids are not that inventive and will really only bother applying for jobs where there is actually some kind of on-campus recruiting event. Kids at good colleges have enough choices of good jobs from the on-campus employers that they rarely bother reaching out to employers that don't come to campus.

You can either participate in this madness, by recruiting on campus, which is a good thing, don't get me wrong, or you can subvert it, by trying to get great kids a year or two *before* they graduate.

I've had a lot of success doing it that way at Fog Creek. The process starts every September, when I start using all my resources to track down the best computer science students in the country. I send letters to a couple of hundred Computer Science departments. I track down lists of CS majors who are, at that point, two years away from graduating (usually you have to know someone in the department, a professor or student, to find these lists). Then I write a personal letter to every single CS major that I can find. Not email, a real piece of paper on Fog Creek letterhead, which I sign myself in actual ink. Apparently, this is rare enough that it gets a *lot* of attention. I tell them we have internships and personally invite them to apply. I send email to CS professors and CS alumni, who usually have some kind of CS-majors mailing list that they forward it on to.

Eventually, we get a lot of applications for these internships, and we can have our pick of the crop. In the last couple of years, I've gotten 200 applications for every internship. We'll generally winnow that pile of applications down to about 10 (per opening) and then call all those people for a phone interview. Of the people getting past the phone interview, we'll probably fly two or three out to New York for an in-person interview.

By the time of the in-person interview, there's such a high probability that we're going to want to hire this person that it's time to launch into full-press *recruitment*. They're met at the airport here by a uniformed limo driver who grabs their luggage and whisks them away to their hotel, probably the coolest hotel they've ever seen in their life, right in the middle of the fashion district with models walking in and out at all hours and complicated bathroom fixtures that are probably a part of the permanent collection of the Museum of Modern Art, but good luck trying to figure out how to brush your teeth. Waiting in the hotel room, we leave a hospitality package with a T-shirt, a suggested walking tour of New York written by Fog Creek staffers, and a DVD documentary of the 2005 summer interns.[2] There's a DVD player in the room, so a lot of them watch how much fun was had by previous interns.

After a day of interviews, we invite the students to stay in New York at our expense for a couple of days if they want to check out the city, before the limo picks them up at their hotel and takes them back to the airport for their flight home.

Even though only about one in three applicants who make it to the in-person interview stage passes all our interviews, it's really important that the ones who *do* pass have a positive experience. Even the ones who don't make it go back to campus thinking we're a classy employer and tell all their friends how much fun they had staying in a luxury hotel in the Big Apple, which makes their friends apply for an internship the next summer, if only for the chance at the trip.

During the summer of the internship itself, the students generally start out thinking, "OK, it's a nice summer job and some good experience and maybe, just *maybe,* it'll lead to a full-time job." We're a little bit ahead of them.

---

2. You can order a copy of this movie, made by filmmaker Lerone D. Wilson, at www.projectaardvark.com/movie. It's called *Aardvark'd: Twelve Weeks with Geeks.*

We're going to use the summer to decide if we want them as a full-time employee, and they're going to use the summer to decide if they want to work for us.

So we give them real work. Hard work. Our interns always work on production code. Sometimes they're working on the coolest new stuff in the company, which can make the permanent employees a little jealous, but that's life. One summer we had a team of four interns build a whole new product, Fog Creek Copilot (check it out at copilot.com), from the ground up. That internship paid for itself in a matter of months. Even when they're not building a new product, they're working on real, shipping code, with some major area of functionality that they are totally, personally responsible for (with experienced mentors to help out, of course).

And then we make sure they have a great time. We host parties and open houses. We get them free housing in a rather nice local dorm where they can make friends from other companies and schools. We have some kind of extra-curricular activity or field trip every week: Broadway musicals (this year they went crazy about *Avenue Q*), movie openings, museum tours, a boat ride around Manhattan, a Yankees game, and believe it or not one of this year's favorite things was a trip to Top of the Rock. I mean, it's just a tall building where you go out on the roof in the middle of Manhattan. You wouldn't think it would be such an awe-inspiring experience. But it was. A few Fog Creek employees go along on each activity, too.

At the end of the summer, there are always a few interns who convinced us that they are the truly great kinds of programmers that we just have to hire. Not all of them, mind you—some are merely great programmers that we are willing to pass on, and others would be great somewhere else, but not at Fog Creek. For example, we're a fairly autonomous company without a lot of middle management, where people are expected to be completely self-driven. Historically, a couple of times we hired a summer intern who would have be great in a situation where they had someone to guide them, but at Fog Creek they didn't get enough direction and floundered.

Anyway, for the ones we really want to hire, there's no use in waiting. We make an early offer for a full-time job, conditional on their graduating. And it's a great offer. We want them to be able to go back to school, compare notes with their friends, and realize that they're getting a higher starting salary than anyone else.

Does this mean we're overpaying? Not at all. You see, the average first year salary has to take into account a certain amount of risk that the person won't work out. But we've already auditioned these kids, and there's no risk that they won't be great. We know what they can do. So when we hire them, we have more information about them than any other employer who has only interviewed them. That means we can pay them more money. We have better information, so we're willing to pay more than employers without that information.

If we've done our job right, and we usually have, by this point the intern completely gives up and accepts our offer. Sometimes it takes a little more persuading. Sometimes they want to leave their options open, but the outstanding offer from Fog Creek ensures that the first time they have to wake up at 8:00 a.m. and put on a suit for an interview with Oracle, when the alarm goes off, there's a good chance that they'll say "Why the heck am I getting up at 8:00 a.m. and putting on a suit for an interview with Oracle when I already have an excellent job waiting for me at Fog Creek?" And, my hope is, they won't even bother going to that interview.

By the way, before I move on, I need to clarify something about internships in computer science and software development. In this day and age, in this country, it is totally expected that these are *paid* internships, and the salaries are usually pretty competitive. Although unpaid internships are common in other fields from publishing to music, we pay $750 a week, plus free housing, plus free lunch, plus free subway passes, not to mention relocation expenses and all the benefits. The dollar amount is a little bit lower than average, but it includes the free housing so it works out being a little bit better than average. I thought I'd mention that because every time I've talked about internships on my website, somebody inevitably gets confused and thinks I'm taking advantage of slave labor or something. You there—young whippersnapper! Get me a frosty cold orange juice, hand-squeezed, and make it snappy!

An internship program creates a pipeline for great employees, but it's a pretty long pipeline, and a lot of people get lost along the way. We basically calculate that we're going to have to hire two interns for every full-time employee that we get out of it, and if you hire interns with one year left in school, there's still a two-year pipeline between when you start hiring and when they show up for their first day of full-time work. That means we hire just about as many interns as we can physically fit in our offices each summer. The first three summers, we tried to limit our internship program to students with one year left in school, but this summer we finally realized that we were missing out on some great younger students, so we opened the program to students in any year in college. Believe it or not, I'm even trying to figure out how to get high school kids in here, maybe setting up computers after school for college money, just to start to build a connection with the next generation of great programmers, even if it becomes a six-year pipeline. I have a long horizon.

Build the Community (*Hard)

The idea here is to create a large community of like-minded smart developers who cluster around your company, somehow, so you have an automatic audience to reach out to every time you have an opening.

This is, to tell the truth, how we found so many of our great Fog Creek people: through my personal website, *Joel on Software* (joelonsoftware.com). Articles on that site can be read by as many as a million people, most of them software developers in some capacity. With a large, self-selecting audience, whenever I mention that I'm looking for someone on the home page, I'll usually get a pretty big pile of very good resumes.

This is that category with the asterisk that means "hard," since I feel like I'm giving you advice that says, "To win a beauty pageant, (a) get beautiful, and (b) enter the pageant." That's because I'm really not sure why or how my site became so popular or why the people who read it are the best software developers.

I really wish I could help you more here. Derek Powazek wrote a good book on the subject.[3] A lot of companies tried various blogging strategies, and unfortunately a lot of them failed to build up any kind of audience, so all I can say is that what worked for us may or may not work for you, and I'm not sure what you can do about it.

Employee Referrals: May Be Slippery When Wet

The standard bit of advice on finding great software developers is to ask your existing

---

3. Derek Powazek, *Design for Community: The Art of Connecting Real People in Virtual Places* (Berkeley, CA: New Riders, 2001).

developers. The theory is, gosh, they're smart developers, they must know other smart developers.

And they might, but they also have very dear friends who are not very good developers, and there are about a million land mines in this field, so the truth is I generally consider the idea of employee referrals to be one of the weakest sources of new hires.

One big risk, of course, is noncompete agreements. If you didn't think these mattered, think about the case of a company called Crossgain, which had to fire a quarter of its employees, all ex-Microsoft, when Microsoft threatened them with individual lawsuits.[4] No programmer in their right mind should ever sign a noncompete agreement, but most of them do because they can never imagine that it would be enforced, or because they are not in the habit of reading contracts, or because they already accepted the employment offer and moved their families across the country and the first day of work is the first time they've seen this agreement and it's a little bit too late to try to negotiate it. So they

---

4. Jay Greene, "Crossgain vs. Microsoft: 'Mooning the Giant,'" *Business Week* (February 5, 2001). An archived copy is available on the Web at www.businessweek.com/2001/01_06/b3718158.htm.

sign, but this is one of the slimiest practices of employers, and they *are* often enforceable and enforced.

The point being, noncompete agreements may mean that if you rely too heavily on referrals and end up hiring a block of people from the same ex-employer, which is where your employees know the other star programmers from in the *first* place, you're taking a pretty major risk.

Another problem is that if you have any kind of selective hiring process at all, when you ask your employees to find referrals, they're not going to even consider telling you about their real friends. Nobody wants to persuade their friends to apply for a job at their company only to get rejected. It sort of puts a damper on the friendship.

Since they won't tell you about their friends, and you may not be able to hire the people they used to work with, what's left is not very many potential referrals.

But the *real* problem with employee referrals is what happens when recruiting managers with a rudimentary understanding of economics decide to offer cash bonuses for these referrals. This is quite common. The rationale goes like this: it can cost $30,000 to $50,000 to hire someone good through a headhunter or outside recruiter. If we can pay our employees, say, a $5,000 bonus for every hire they bring in, or maybe an expensive sports car for every ten referrals, or whatever, think how much money that will save? And $5,000 sounds like a fortune to a salaried employee, because it is. So this sounds like a win-win kind of situation.

The trouble is that suddenly you can see the little gears turning, and employees start dragging in everyone they can think of for interviews, and they have a real strong incentive to get these people hired, so they coach them for the interview, and Quiet Conversations are held in conference rooms with the interviewers, and suddenly your entire workforce is trying to get you to hire someone's useless college roommate.

And it doesn't work. A dotcom boom-and-bust company called ArsDigita got a lot of publicity for buying a Ferrari and putting it in the parking lot and announcing that anyone who got ten referrals could have it. Nobody ever got close, the quality of new hires went down, and the company fell apart, but probably not because of the Ferrari, which, it turns out, was rented, and not much more than a publicity stunt, although apparently the executives were not above taking it out for a spin once in a while.

When a Fog Creek employee suggests someone that might be perfect to work for us, we'll be willing to skip the initial phone screen, but that's *it*. We still want them going through all the same interviews and we maintain the same high standards, and we don't offer a bonus for referrals.

Chapter 3

A FIELD GUIDE TO DEVELOPERS

Unfortunately, you can advertise in all the right places, have a fantastic internship program, and interview all you want, but if the great programmers don't want to work for you, they ain't gonna come work for you. So this section will serve as a kind of field guide to developers: what they're looking for, what they like and dislike in a workplace, and what it's going to take to be a top choice for top developers.

Private Offices

Last year I went to a Computer Science conference at Yale. One of the speakers, a Silicon Valley veteran who had founded or led quite an honor roll of venture-capital funded startups, held up the book *Peopleware*.[1]

"You have to read this book," he said. "This is the bible of how to run a software company. This is the most important book out there for how to run software companies."

I had to agree with him: *Peopleware* is a great book. One of the most important, and most controversial, topics in that book is that you have to give programmers lots of quiet space, probably private offices, if you want them to be productive. The authors, DeMarco and Lister, go on and on about that subject.

After the speech, I went up to the speaker. "I agree with you about *Peopleware*," I said. "Tell me: did you have private offices for your developers at all your startups?"

"Of course not," he said. "The VCs would never go for that."

Hmm.

"But that might be the number one most important thing in that book," I said.

"Yeah, but you gotta pick your battles. To VCs, private offices look like you're wasting their money."

---

1. Tom DeMarco and Timothy Lister, *Peopleware: Productive Projects and Teams, Second Edition* (New York: Dorset House, 1999).

There's a strong culture in Silicon Valley that requires you to jam a lot of programmers into a big open space, despite a preponderance of evidence that giving them private offices is far more productive. I'm not really getting through to people, it seems, because programmers kind of *like* being social, even if it means they are unproductive, so it's an uphill battle.

I've even heard programmers say things like, "Yeah, we all work in cubicles, but *everyone* works in a cubicle—up to and including the CEO!"

"The CEO? Does the CEO really work in a cubicle?"

"Well, he *has* a cubicle, but actually now that you mention it, there's this one conference room that he goes to for all his important meetings..."

Mmmm hmmm. A fairly common Silicon Valley phenomenon is the CEO who makes a big show of working from a cubicle just like the hoi polloi, although somehow there's this one conference room that he tends to make his own ("Only when there's something private to be discussed," he'll claim, but half the time when you walk by that conference room there's your CEO, all by himself, talking on the phone to his golf buddy, with his Cole Haans up on the conference table).

Anyway, I don't want to revisit the discussion of why private offices make software developers more productive,[2, 3, 4] or why just putting on headphones with music to drown out the ambient noise reduces the ability of programmers to have useful insights,[5] and why it doesn't really cost that much more in the scheme of things to have private offices for developers.[6]

Today I'm talking about recruiting, and private offices in recruiting.

No matter what you think about productivity, and no matter what you think about egalitarian workspaces, two things are incontrovertible:

---

2. Tom DeMarco and Tim Lister, "Programmer Performance and the Effects of the Workplace," *Proceedings of the 8th International Conference on Software Engineering* (London: IEEE Computer Society Press, 1985).

3. Capers Jones, "How Office Space Affects Programming Productivity," *IEEE Computer* 28, no. 1 (January 1995), pp. 7676.

4. Gerald M. McCue, "IBM's Santa Teresa Laboratory— Architectural design for program development," *IBM Systems Journal* 17, no. 1 (1978).

5. Tom DeMarco and Tim Lister, *Peopleware Second Edition*, p. 78ff.

6. Joel Spolsky, "Bionic Office," published at www. joelonsoftware.com on September 23, 2003 (search for "Bionic").

1. Private offices have higher status.

2. Cubicles and other shared space can be socially awkward.

Given these two facts, the bottom line is that programmers are more likely to take the job that offers them a private office. Especially if there's a door that shuts, and a window, and a nice view.

Now, it's an unfortunate fact that some of these things that make recruiting easier are not really within your power. Even CEOs and founders can be prevented from establishing private offices if they're dependent on VCs. Most companies only move or rearrange their office space every five to ten years. Smaller startups may not be able to afford private offices. So my experience has been that a number of excuses all pile up until it's virtually impossible to get private offices for developers in any but the most enlightened of companies, and even in those companies, the decision of where to move and where people should work is often taken once every ten years by a committee consisting of the office manager's secretary and a junior associate from a big architecture firm, who is apt to believe architecture-school fairy tales about how "open spaces mean open companies," or whatever, with darn-near zero input from the developers or the development team.

This is something of a scandal, and I'll keep fighting the good fight, but in the meantime, private offices are *not* impossible; we've managed to do it for all of our full-time programmers, most of the time, even in New York City, where the rents are the highest in the country, and there's no question that it makes people much happier about working at Fog Creek, so if you all want to keep resisting, *so be it,* I'll just let this remain a competitive advantage for me.

The Physical Workspace

There's more to the physical workspace than private offices. When a candidate comes to your company for the day of interviews, they're going to look around at where people are working, and try to imagine themselves working there. If the office space is pleasant, if it's bright, if it's in a nice neighborhood, and if everything is new and clean, they'll have happy thoughts. If the office space is crowded, if the carpets are ratty and the walls haven't been painted and there are posters up with pictures of rowing teams and the word TEAMWORK in large print, they're going to have Dilbert thoughts.

A lot of tech people are remarkably unaware of the general condition of their office. In fact, even people who are otherwise attuned to the benefits of a nice office may be blinded to the particular weaknesses of their own office, since they're so used to it.

Put yourself in your candidate's heads, and think honestly:

- What will they think of our location? How does Buffalo sound, compared to, say, Austin? Do people really want to move to Detroit? If you're in Buffalo or Detroit, can you at least try to do most of your interviewing in September?

- When they get to the office, what is the experience like? What do they see? Do they see a clean and exciting place? Is there a nice atrium lobby with live palm trees and a fountain, or does it feel like a government dental clinic in a slum, with dying corn plants and old copies of *Newsweek*?

- What does the workspace look like? Is everything new and shiny? Or do you still have that gigantic, yellowing TEAM BANANA sign up, the one that was printed on fanfold paper on a dot matrix printer back when there used to be a thing called fanfold paper and a thing called dot matrix printers?

- What do the desks look like? Do programmers have multiple large flat screens or a single CRT? Are the chairs Aerons or Staples Specials?

Let me, for a moment, talk about the famous Aeron chair, made by Herman Miller. They cost about $900. This is about $800 more than a cheap office chair from Office Depot or Staples.

They are *much* more comfortable than cheap chairs. If you get the right size and adjust it properly, most people can sit in them all day long without feeling uncomfortable. The back and seat are made out of a kind of mesh that lets air flow so you don't get sweaty. The ergonomics, especially of the newer models with lumbar support, are excellent.

They last longer than cheap chairs. We've been in business for six years, and every Aeron is literally in mint condition: I challenge anyone to see the difference between the chairs we bought in 2000 and the chairs we bought three months ago. They easily last for ten years. The cheap chairs literally start falling apart after a matter of months. You'll need at least four $100 chairs to last as long as an Aeron.

So the bottom line is that an Aeron only really costs $500 more over ten years, or $50 a year. One dollar per week per programmer.

A nice roll of toilet paper runs about a buck. Your programmers are probably using about one roll a week, each.

So upgrading them to an Aeron chair literally costs the same amount as you're spending on their *toilet paper,* and I assure you that if you tried to bring up toilet paper in the budget committee you would be sternly told not to mess around; there were important things to discuss.

The Aeron chair has, sadly, been tarnished with a reputation of being extravagant, especially for startups. It somehow came to stand for the symbol of all the VC money that was wasted in the dotcom boom, which is a shame, because it's not very expensive when you consider how long it lasts; indeed, when you think of the eight hours a day you spend sitting in it, even the top of the line model, with the lumbar support and the friggin' *tailfins*, is so dang cheap you practically *make* money by buying them.

Toys

Similar logic applies for other developer toys. There is simply no reason not to get your developers top-of-the-line computers, at least two large (21") LCD screens (or one 30" screen), and give them free rein on Amazon.com to order any technical book they want. These are obvious productivity gains, but more importantly to our discussion here, they're crucial recruiting tools, especially in a world where most companies treat programmers as interchangeable cogs, typists, really, why do you need such a big monitor and what's wrong with 15" CRTs? When *I* was a kid, ...

The Social Life of Developers

Software developers are not really all that different from regular people. Sure, I know, it's popular these days to think of developers as stereotypical Asperger's geeks, totally untuned to interpersonal things, but that's just not true, and even Asperger's geeks care about the social aspect of a workspace, which includes these issues:

How Are Programmers Treated Inside the Organization?

Are they hotshots or typists? Is company management made up of engineers or former programmers? When developers go to a conference, do they fly first class? (I don't care if that seems like a waste of money. Stars go first class. Get used to it.) When they fly in for an interview, does a limo pick them up at the airport, or are they expected to find their own way to the office? All else being equal, developers are going to prefer an organization that treats them like stars. If your CEO is a grouchy ex-sales person who doesn't understand why these prima donna developers keep demanding things like wrist pads and big monitors and comfortable chairs, who do they think they are?, your company probably needs an attitude adjustment. You're not going to get great developers if you don't respect them.

Who Are Their Colleagues?

One thing programmers pay close attention to in the day of interviewing is the people they meet. Are they nice? More importantly: are they smart? I did a summer internship once at Bellcore, a spinoff of Bell Labs, and everybody I met kept telling me the same thing, again and again: "The great thing about working for Bellcore is the people."

That said, if you have any grouchy developers that you just can't get rid of, at least take them off the interview schedule, and if you have cheerful, social, cruise-director types, make sure they're on it. Keep reminding yourself that when your candidate goes home and has to make a decision about where to work, if everyone they met was glum, they are not going to have such a positive memory of your company.

By the way, the original hiring rule for Fog Creek, stolen from Microsoft, was "Smart, and Gets Things Done." Even before we started the company, we realized that we should add a third rule: "Not a jerk."[7] In retrospect, at Microsoft, not being a jerk is *not* a requirement to get the job; although I'm sure they would pay lip service to how important it is for people to be nice to one another, the bottom line is that they would never disqualify someone for a job just because they were a jerk, in fact, being a jerk sometimes seems like a *prerequisite* for getting into upper management. This doesn't really seem to hurt from a business perspective, although it does hurt from a recruiting perspective. Who wants to work at a company where jerks are tolerated?

Independence and Autonomy

When I quit my job at Juno, back in 1999, before starting Fog Creek Software, HR gave me a standard exit interview, and somehow, I fell into the trap of telling the HR person everything that was wrong about the management of the company, something which I knew perfectly well could have no possible benefit to me and could only, actually, hurt, but I did it anyway,

---

7. Robert I. Sutton, *The No Asshole Rule: Building a Civilized Workplace and Surviving One That Isn't* (New York: Warner Business Books, 2007).

and the main thing I complained about was Juno's style of hit-and-run management. Most of the time, you see, managers would leave people alone to quietly get their work done, but occasionally, they would get themselves involved in some microscopic detail of something which they would insist be done exactly their way, no excuses, and then they'd move on to micromanage some other task, not staying around long enough to see the farcical results. For example, I remember a particularly annoying period of two or three days where everyone from my manager to the CEO got involved in telling me exactly how dates must be entered on the Juno signup questionnaire. They weren't trained as UI designers and didn't spend enough time talking to me about the issues to understand why I happened to be right in that particular case, but it didn't matter: management just would not back down on that issue and wouldn't even take the time to listen to my arguments. The decision was made in a meeting with the CEO *that I wasn't told about.*

Basically, if you're going to hire smart people, you're going to have to let them apply their skills to their work. Managers can advise, which they're welcome to do, but they must be extremely careful to avoid having their "advice" interpreted as a command, since on any given technical issue it's likely that management knows less than the workers in the trenches, especially, as I said, if you're hiring good people.

Developers want to be hired for their skills, and treated as experts, and allowed to make decisions within their own realm of expertise.

No Politics

Actually, politics happen everywhere that three or more people congregate, and it can be completely harmless. What I really mean by "no politics" is "no dysfunctional politics." Programmers have very well-honed senses of justice. Code either works, or it doesn't. There's no sense in arguing whether a bug exists, since you can test the code and find out. The world of programming is very just and very strictly ordered, and a heck of a lot of people go into programming in the first place because they prefer to spend their time in a just, orderly place: a strict meritocracy where you can win any debate simply by being *right*.

And this is the kind of environment you have to create to attract programmers. When a programmer complains about "politics," they mean—very precisely—any situation in which personal considerations outweigh technical considerations. Nothing is more infuriating than when a developer is told to use a certain programming language, not the best one for the task at hand, because the boss likes it. Nothing is more maddening than when people are promoted because of their ability to network rather than being promoted strictly on merit. Nothing is more aggravating to a developer than being forced to do something that is technically inferior because someone higher than them in the organization, or someone better-connected, insists on it.

Nothing is more satisfying than winning an argument on its technical merits even when you should have lost it on political merits. When I started working at Microsoft, there was a major, misguided project underway called MacroMan to create a graphical macro programming language. The programming language would have been very frustrating for real programmers, because the graphical nature didn't really give you a way to implement loops or conditionals, but would not have really helped nonprogrammers, who, I think, are just not used to thinking in algorithms and wouldn't have understood MacroMan in the first place. When I complained about MacroMan, my boss told me, "Nothing's gonna derail *that* train. Give up." But I kept arguing, and arguing, and arguing—I was fresh out of college, about as unconnected as anyone could be at Microsoft—and eventually people listened to the meat of my arguments and the MacroMan project was shut down. It didn't matter who I was, it mattered that I was right. That's the kind of nonpolitical organization that delights programmers.

All in all, focusing on the social dynamics of your organization is crucial to making a healthy, pleasant place to work that will retain programmers and attract programmers.

What Am I Working On?

To some extent, one of the best ways you can attract developers is to let them work on something interesting.

This may be the hardest thing to change: doggone it, if you're in the business of making software for the gravel and sand industry, that's the business you're in, and you can't pretend to be some cool web startup just to attract developers.

Developers also like working on something simple enough or popular enough that they can explain to Aunt Irma, at Thanksgiving. Aunt Irma, of course, being a nuclear physicist, doesn't really know that much about Ruby programming in the gravel and sand industry, but she is excited by fluid dynamics simulators.

Finally, many developers are going to look at the social values of the company they're working for. Jobs at social networking companies and blog companies help bring people together and don't really pollute, it seems, so they're popular, while jobs in the munitions industry or in ethically challenged accounting-fraud-ridden companies are a lot less popular.

Unfortunately, I'm not really sure if I can think of any way for the average hiring manager to do anything about this. You can try to change your product lineup to make something "cool," but that's just not going to go very far. There are a few things, though, that I've seen companies do in this area:

Let the Top Recruits Pick Their Own Project

For many years, Oracle Corporation had a program called MAP: the "Multiple Alternatives Program." This was offered to the college graduates whom they considered the top candidates from each class. The idea was that they could come to Oracle, spend a week or two looking around, visiting all the groups with openings, and then choose any opening they wanted to work in.

Google also gives programmers an enormous amount of leeway in what they work on; they have a concept called 20% time, which allows anyone to devote 20% of their time to any project they want, without getting anyone's approval.

Use Cool New Technologies Unnecessarily

The big investment banks in New York are considered fairly tough places for programmers. The working conditions are dreadful, with long hours, noisy environments, and tyrannical bosses; programmers are very distinct third-class citizens, while the testosterone-crazed apes who actually sell and trade financial instruments are corporate royalty, with $30,000,000 bonuses and all the cheeseburgers they can eat (often delivered by a programmer who happened to be nearby). That's the stereotype, anyway, so to keep the best developers, investment banks have two strategies: paying a ton of money, and allowing programmers basically free rein to keep rewriting everything over and over again in whatever hot new programming language they feel like learning. Wanna rewrite that whole trading app in Ruby? Whatever. Just get me a goddamned cheeseburger.

Some programmers couldn't care less about what programming language they're using, but most would just love to have the opportunity to work with exciting new technologies. Today that may be Python or Ruby on Rails; three years ago it was C# and before that Java.

Now, I'm not telling you not to use the best tool for the job, and I'm not telling you to rewrite in the hot *language-du-jour* every two years, but if you can find ways for developers to get experience with newer languages, frameworks, and technologies, they'll be happier. Even if you don't dare rewrite your core application, is there any reason your internal tools, or less-critical new applications, can't be written in an exciting new language as a learning project?

Can I Identify with the Company?

Most programmers aren't just looking for a gig to pay the rent. They don't want a "day job": they want to feel like their work has meaning. They want to identify with their company. Young programmers, especially, are attracted to ideological companies. A lot of companies have

some connection to open source or the free software movement, and that can be attractive to
idealistic developers. Other companies line up
with social causes, or produce a product which,
in some way, can be perceived or framed as ben-
efitting society.

As a recruiter, your job is to identify the idealistic aspects of your company, and make sure
candidates are aware of them.

Some companies even strive to create their
own ideological movements. Chicago-area
startup 37signals has strongly aligned themselves with the idea of simplicity: simple, easy to
use apps like Backpack and the simple, easy to
use programming framework Ruby on Rails.

For 37signals, simplicity is an "-ism," practically an international political movement.
Simplicity is not just simplicity, oh no, it's sum-
mertime, it's beautiful music and peace and
justice and happiness and pretty girls with flow-
ers in their hair. David Heinemeier Hansson, the
creator of Rails, says that their story is "one of
beauty, happiness, and motivation. Taking pride
and pleasure in your work and in your tools.
That story simply isn't a fad, it's a trend. A story
that allows for words like passion and enthusi-
asm to be part of the sanctioned vocabulary of
developers without the need to make excuses for
yourself. Or feel embarrassed about really liking

what you do."[8] Elevating a web programming framework to a thing of "beauty, happiness, and motivation" may seem like hubris, but it's very appealing and sure differentiates their company. In propagating the narrative of Ruby on Rails as Happiness, they're practically guaranteeing that at least some developers out there will be looking for Ruby on Rails jobs.

But 37signals is still new at this identity management campaign thing. They don't hold a *candle* to Apple Computer, which, with a single Super Bowl ad in 1984, managed to cement their position *to this day* as the countercultural force of freedom against dictatorship, of liberty against oppression, of colors against black and white, of pretty women in bright red shorts against brainwashed men in suits. The implications of this, I'm afraid, are ironically Orwellian: giant corporations manipulating their public image in a way which doesn't even make sense (like, uh, they're a computer company—what the hell does that have to do with being against dictatorships?) and successfully creating a culture of identity that has computer shoppers around the world feeling like they're not just buying a computer, they're *buying into*

---

8. David Heinemeier Hansson, "Rails steps into year three," www.loudthinking.com/arc/000594.html, August 6, 2006.

a movement. When you buy an iPod, of course, you're supporting Gandhi against British Colonialism. Every MacBook you buy takes a stand against dictatorship and hunger!

Anyway. Deep breath.... The real point of this section is to think of what your company stands for, how it's perceived, and how it could be perceived. Managing your corporate brand is just as important for recruiting as it is for marketing.

One Thing That Programmers Don't Care About

They don't care about money, actually, unless you're screwing up on the other things. If you start to hear complaints about salaries where you never heard them before, that's usually a sign that people aren't really loving their job. If potential new hires just won't back down on their demands for outlandish salaries, you're probably dealing with a case of people who are thinking, "Well, if it's going to have to suck to go to work, at least I should be getting paid well."

That doesn't mean you can underpay people, because they do care about justice, and they will get infuriated if they find out that different people are getting different salaries for the same work, or that everyone in your shop is making 20% less than an otherwise identical shop down the road, and suddenly money will be a big issue. You do have to pay competitively, but all said, of all the things that programmers look at in deciding where to work, as long as the salaries are basically fair, they will be surprisingly low on their list of considerations, and offering high salaries is a surprisingly ineffective tool in overcoming problems like the fact that programmers get 15" monitors and salespeople yell at them all the time and the job involves making nuclear weapons out of baby seals.

Chapter 4

SORTING RESUMES

The standard job application, a cover letter and a resume, is a phenomenally weak way to introduce a candidate. It gives you only the faintest clues as to the quality of an applicant.

Sometimes, though, a resume gives pretty strong *negative* clues that allow you to screen out applicants without going much further. Once I got a resume from someone who claimed to be an expert in Microsoft Window [*sic*] programming. Another time the only experience listed on the application was a job at Dunkin' Donuts. That resume did a pretty good job of following all the suggestions that high school career-guidance advisors love to give out (this guy "managed trays of donuts"), but there was not a smidgen of evidence that the applicant had ever seen a computer.

Other than that, though, it can be extremely hard to tell much about a candidate from a resume. Our policy at Fog Creek, then, has three parts:

1. We try to be selective about how we advertise our jobs, so as to limit the amount of noise in the resume pile.

2. We certainly don't hire based on resumes; we only screen *out* based on resumes to reduce the number of people whom we have to interview.

3. In order to sort the remaining resumes to decide what order to interview people, we use a strictly objective system of reviewing and scoring them, so at least we are being fair and consistent in our interpretation of that very weak signal that comes from resumes.

Criteria for Sorting Resumes

There are several fairly objective measures that we look at. Again, this is *solely for the purpose of sorting resumes,* so that the first people we call are the ones who are most likely to work out.

Passion

We look for evidence that the applicant is passionate about computers and really loves programming. Typical evidence of this:

- Jobs with computers or experience programming going back to a very early age. Great programmers are more likely to have spent a summer at computer camp, or building an online appointment scheduler for their uncle the dentist, rather than working at Banana Republic folding clothes.

- Extra-curricular activities. People who love programming often work on their own programming projects (or contribute to an open source project) in their spare time.

- Waxing rhapsodic in their cover letter about how they were moved to tears by *Structure and Interpretation of Computer Programs*.[1]

---

1. Hal Abelson and Gerald Jay Sussman, *Structure and Interpretation of Computer Programs* (Cambridge, MA: MIT Press, 1985). Second Edition, 1996.

- Sometimes certain programming languages or technologies on a resume indicate evidence of someone who loves programming enough to explore new technologies. At the time I'm writing this, seeing Ruby on a resume is a good sign of the kind of programmer who loves to check out the latest thing and try to improve their skills because they're passionate about programming, because not so many employers are really demanding Ruby yet. You have to be careful here; in 1996, Java on a resume was a sign of the same passion, but today it adds almost no information.

Pickiness

We look closely at the cover letter for evidence that the applicant really wants to work for *us*. We don't want to see a generic cover letter talking about me, me, me: we want to see a coherent argument as to why they've thought about this seriously and concluded that Fog Creek is the place they want to work. There are two reasons for using this as a clue. First, it's a sign that the candidate is not applying to hundreds of jobs at the same time. The fact that they took the time to learn about Fog Creek and wrote a custom cover letter just for us means that they have a lot of confidence in their abilities, so they're applying to a select few employers, not bulk mailing a thousand. A bulk-mailed resume can be a symptom of desperation. More importantly, a custom cover letter is a sign that if we *do* make this candidate an offer, they're likely to accept it. That improves our yield. If I only have time to interview six people, all else being equal, I'd rather interview six people who really want to work for Fog Creek, not generic smart people who are also applying to a hundred other jobs. All else being equal.

English

Scoring resumes by English skills was a hard decision for us to make, because computer programming is one of those fields where an immigrant who doesn't speak English can still be a brilliant programmer. That said, years of experience working with programmers have taught me that programmers who can communicate their ideas clearly are going to be far, far more effective than programmers who can only really communicate well with the compiler. It is crucial for documenting code, it is crucial for writing specifications and technical design documents that other people can review, and it's crucial even for those meetings where you sit around discussing how to do something best: brilliant programmers who have trouble explaining their ideas just can't make as much of a contribution. In this particular category, we also consider the neatness and orderliness of their resume. A disorganized resume rife with grammatical errors where nothing lines up is a pretty big red flag for a disorganized thinker or just general sloppiness; for many jobs this can be fine, but not for software development. In particular, we usually completely disqualify resumes that are full of English mistakes. It's not that hard, even for a nonnative speaker, to find someone to check your resume, and failure to do that usually reflects a profound lack of concern over the quality of the things that you do. That said, we try to be considerate of nonnative speakers who are nonetheless excellent communicators: leaving out articles in charming Eastern European way, or starting every paragraph with "So" in the charming Pacific Northwestian way, is not a showstopper.

Brains

In this category we're looking for evidence that a candidate is, well, smart, or at least the kind of nerdy brainiac who went to math camp. Signs of this include high GPAs, high standardized test scores, honors societies like Phi Beta Kappa, people who participate in Top Coder competitions, play competitive chess, or go to ACM Programming contests.

Selectivity

Another thing we look for on resumes is evidence that someone has gone through some highly selective process in the past. Not everyone at Ivy League schools is worth hiring, and not everyone at community college is worth avoiding, but getting into a very selective school does at least mean that *someone, somewhere* judged you using some kind of selection process and decided that you were pretty smart. Our company criterion for selectivity is usually getting into a school or program that accepts less than 30% of its applicants (there are about 60 schools in the US that meet this standard), or working for a company that is known to have a difficult application process, like a whole day of interviews. Getting into highly selective courses in the military (e.g., officer's training, pilot's school, etc.) or getting into highly selective units like the Marines, indicates someone who has made it through some kind of difficult application/selection procedure, and all in all this is a positive sign.

Hard-Core

For experienced programmers, there are certain technologies that are considered somewhat more hard-core than others, simply because they are, well, harder to do well. Again, this is a pretty weak indicator, but all else being equal, I'm more impressed by someone who has done work in OCaml than someone who has worked in Java. Assembler or device-driver or kernel work is somewhat more impressive than Visual Basic or PHP. C++ with ATL is harder than Perl. People who have worked on operating systems or compilers are more hard-core than people who have worked on simple database front-ends.

I'm sure that this will be seen as incendiary; after all, most of my personal programming experience in the past five years is with VBScript, which is sort of like a version of Visual Basic dumbed down for people with severe brain trauma. Remember again that I said that resumes are a very weak way of judging programmers, and you only get the faintest signals from them; that said, some technologies are just *harder* than other technologies, and if you happened to have worked with them successfully, there's a smidgen more evidence that you might be the right person to hire, so for the purpose of sorting resumes, difficult technologies tend to float you to the top, while claiming competence in, say, Microsoft Word tends to float you toward the bottom.

Diversity

Before I start a massive flame war of international scope by using the loaded term "diversity," let me carefully define what I mean by this. Specifically, I'm looking for people who come from enough of a different background than the existing team that they are likely to bring new ideas and new ways of thinking to the team and challenge any incipient groupthink that is likely to keep us boxed into our own echo-chamber way of thinking about things. When I say different background, I mean culturally, socially, and professionally. Someone who has a lot of experience with enterprise software may bring useful diversity to a team of Internet programmers. Someone who grew up poor is going to bring useful diversity to a startup full of Andover preppies. A stay-at-home mom rejoining the workplace may bring useful diversity to a team of recent graduates. An electrical engineer with Assembler experience may bring useful diversity to a team of Lisp hackers. A recent college graduate from Estonia may bring useful diversity to a team of experienced management consultants from the Midwest. The only theory here is that the more diverse your team is, the more likely that someone on the team will have some experience in their background that allows them to come up with a different solution.

It is *really, really important* to remember that these categories—Passion, Pickiness, English, Brains, Selectivity, Hard-Core, and Diversity— are *not* hiring criteria. They are just too weak for that. There are way too many excellent people who would score low on this test or poor programmers who would score high. Before you go off ranting about how Joel only thinks you should hire from the Ivy League, or that I have some kind of GPA fetish, or whatnot, it's important to understand that this list is just not a list of reasons to hire someone or reject someone. All it is is an objective and fair way to sort a big pile of resumes to find the candidates who are most likely to work out so that you can interview them first, and *then* decide if they're worth hiring.

If Resumes Are So Weak, Can't We Add Some Other Hoops?

This is certainly not, by any stretch of the imagination, the ideal set of rules for sorting resumes. I'd much rather be able to sort resumes by the candidate's ability to implement a recursive algorithm, how long it takes them to find a bug in code, or whether or not they can keep nine items in short-term memory, all of which are better indicators of success as programmers than things like whether you got past an elite college's admissions committee. Unfortunately, those things aren't on resumes.

One temptation of recruiters is to try and add a few extra hoops to the application process. I've frequently heard the suggestion of including a programming quiz of some sort in the application procedure. This does work, in the sense that it reduces the number of applications you get, but it doesn't work, in the sense that it doesn't really improve the quality. Great developers have enough choices of places to work that only require the usual cover letter/resume application to get started; by inventing artificial hoops and programming tests and whatnot simply to apply, you're just as likely to scare away good programmers as weak programmers. Indeed, you may be more likely to scare away the best programmers, who have the most alternatives, and get left with a pool of fairly desperate candidates who are willing to do extra work to apply simply because they don't have any alternatives.

Don't Look for Experience with Particular Technologies

Once I was on a panel at NYU giving students advice on careers in IT. My advice was that before graduating you should make sure to learn how to write well, maybe by taking a creative writing course, and take a class in Econ so that the business side of the business isn't a mystery.[2] I also recommended at least one low-level programming course in C or Assembler just to help you understand how computers work at a lower level.

---

2. Joel Spolsky, "Advice for Computer Science College Students," published at www.joelonsoftware.com on January 2, 2005 (search for "College Advice").

On the panel with me was a nice chap from a local headhunter, in fact, one of the better tech recruiters in the city. His speech consisted of fifteen minutes of tedious alphabet soup. "We're seeing a lot of XML, some C++, SOAP and WSDL are getting hot, but you're not seeing as much COM or even ATL." And on, and on, until my eyes were spinning. This was a fellow who entirely thought of the world in terms of keywords on resumes.

To top programmers, the most maddening thing about recruiters is their almost morbid fascination with keywords and buzzwords. The entire industry of professional headhunters and recruiters is bizarrely fixated on the simple algorithm of matching candidates to positions by looking for candidates who have the complete list of technology acronyms that the employer happens to be looking for. It becomes especially infuriating to realize that most of these recruiters have no idea what any of these technologies *are*. "Oh, you don't have MSMQ experience? Never mind." At least when real estate agents prattle on about Sub-Zero® refrigerators and Viking stoves, they at least know what these things *are* (although any stainless steel refrigerator counts as "Sub-Zero" these days). The easiest way to catch out a technical recruiter is when they inevitably insist on five years of experience with Ruby on Rails, or refuse to consider someone for a "Windows API" job when they only have "Win32" on their resume.

The reason recruiters do this is because it's easy, it can be computerized, and it's the only way they know how to judge developers.

For almost all software development positions, though, it is the worst possible way to hire.

Our philosophy is that we're hiring for the long term, and any technology you happen to know right now may well be obsolete next year. Furthermore, some of these technologies are very easy to learn. If I needed to hire someone to do Ruby development, someone with extensive Smalltalk and Python experience who had never even *heard* of Ruby would be a lot more likely to be successful than someone who read a book about Ruby once. For someone who is basically a good software developer, learning another programming language is just not going to be a big deal. In two weeks, they'll be pretty productive. In two years, you may need them to do something completely different in a programming language which hasn't even been invented.

The keywords section of a resume can't be trusted much, anyway: every working programmer knows about these computer programs that filter resumes based on keywords, so they usually have a section of their resume containing every technology they have ever touched, solely to get through the filters.

There is, I think, one exception to this rule. If you're hiring an architect or head developer—that is, the chief software engineer who is going to have to lay out the initial code and figure out how things work together—you probably want to hire someone with a lot of experience in the technology that you're using. A team developing GUIs for Windows using C++ and MFC is going to need at least one Windows/MFC guru somewhere on the team who can make sure that the code is organized correctly in the first place and who has enough experience to know how to solve the really hard problems that might come up.

Don't start a new project without at least one architect with several years of solid experience in the language, classes, APIs, and platforms you're building on. If you have a choice of platforms, use the one your team has the most skills with, even if it's not the trendiest or nominally the most productive. Occasionally, this may mean you interview to find a candidate with really extensive experience in a particular set of technologies (not keywords, mind you: the whole stack, such as LAMP or .NET or J2EE). But most of your software developers should not be hired by keyword matching.

Chapter 5

THE PHONE SCREEN

It happens all the time. We get a resume that everyone thinks is really exciting. Terrific grades. All kinds of powerful-sounding jobs. Lots of experience. Speaks seventeen languages. And saved over 10,000 kittens!

Look! Kittens!

And then I call them up, and I can't stand talking to them. Within ten minutes, I realize they are not going to make it as programmers. I've had people with great resumes tell me a pointer should fit in one byte. Sometimes they just can't answer the simplest questions, or you feel like you have to wrestle the answers out of them.

Before moving on to a full-fledged in-person interview, we usually use a phone screen to make sure that we're not wasting time and money on someone who is just seriously not smart.

A phone screen has distinct advantages over a normal in-person interview. First, it's cheap. It takes forty-five minutes to an hour and actually does eliminate about half of the people who looked really, really good on paper.

More importantly, it's more fair.

With a phone interview, because you can't see the person, it's easier to focus on the quality of what they're saying rather than other external factors not relevant to their job, like their appearance or their nervousness. Ever since Malcolm Gladwell wrote *Blink*, I've been terrified of the prospect that we might be judging candidates too quickly based on things that are not relevant to their ability to do their job— their appearance or confidence or height or general nerdy demeanor might make us way more apt to look on everything else that happens during the interview with rose-colored glasses.[1]

The great thing about a phone interview is that it's much harder to form these kinds of snap judgments; you actually have to listen to what the person is saying and decide if that corresponds to what a smart person might say. This isn't completely true, of course: you may have prejudices about certain accents or dialects. But at least you are moderately less susceptible to appearance prejudice.

---

1. Malcolm Gladwell, *Blink: The Power of Thinking Without Thinking* (New York: Little, Brown and Company, 2005).

My phone interviews have three parts. In the first part, I ask the candidate to describe their career history and basically tell me about themselves. This is mainly intended to get them loosened up and feeling comfortable, to eliminate any nervousness, and to let them sort of present themselves the way they want to be presented. During this stage, you should be looking for evidence that the candidate is a problem solver: the kind of person who gets things done. You're also looking for passion. You want people who care about the stuff that they did.

During this part, I'll drill down on two kinds of things: technology and politics.

> **Technology:** If someone tells me that they implemented such-and-such a project, I'll ask detailed questions about the technology they used and how they used it. I'll also ask specifically what role they played. Sole developer? Developer on a team? I'll tend to go into these questions in great detail, because this is where you uncover the people who either didn't know what they were doing, or have made things up, or have exaggerated their own roles. If someone's resume implies that they spent two years coding in Python, for example, I'm going to drill down until I'm pretty

confident that it sounds like they really have two years of Python experience.

Politics: Behind the boring list of past employers on the resume, there's always a story. What I'm looking for is the story of how the candidate handled challenges in the past. I'm looking for people who got things done, even in the face of opposition. I'm looking for people who challenged the status quo, who overcame objections, and who made things happen. So when the resume says, "drove the adoption of .NET," I want to hear what drove means. In detail. When the resume says that they "founded a company," I want to hear everything. Whose idea was it? Who convinced whom? Who did what? Did it work out? Why not?

The second part of the phone screen is the technical problem. I usually ask the same question for years and years before switching it, because this makes it easier to compare candidates. The question is a wide-ranging, open design question: how would you design a data structure or a block of code to do x? Where x is something kind of big and complicated. I usually have a series of questions ready to guide the candidate down a particular path in the design of this data structure or block of code, because it's such a big question, and I can often tell how smart the candidate is by how far they get down that path in a fixed amount of time.

Here are some ideas to get you started:

- How might you design a program that lets people play Monopoly with each other over the Internet?[2]
- What would be a good data structure for a photo editor?
- How would you implement code to operate the elevators in a high rise?
- How would you implement the rendering engine of a web browser?

The ideal question takes something the interviewee is deeply familiar with, but is unlikely to have ever implemented themselves. You want something that can be done over the phone, without too much writing, so "How would you write the code for quicksort?" is a bad question, because we don't expect programmers to be able to recite code over the phone. You want to have a conversation about algorithms and data structures, really, the meat and potatoes of programming, where the goal is not to find the best

2. Reg Braithwaite, "My favourite interview question," weblog.raganwald.com/2006/06/my-favourite-interview-question.html, June 12, 2006.

possible answer, necessarily, but simply to give you the opportunity to talk about code, to talk about time/space tradeoffs, to talk about performance characteristics of code, all of which will add up to giving you a pretty good idea in your mind whether the person you're talking to is actually pretty good at programming and whether they're smart or not. If you find yourself explaining everything three times, either you're terrible at explaining things, or you're talking to someone who is not that smart.

The bottom line in my interviewing technique is that smart people can generally tell if they're talking to other smart people by having a conversation with them on a difficult or highly technical subject, and the interview question is really just a pretext to have a conversation on a difficult subject so that the interviewer's judgment can form an opinion on whether this is a smart person or not.

The third and final part of the interview is letting the candidate interview me.

By this point, I've already decided if this person seems smart enough to score an in-person interview. So I treat the third part of the phone interview as if I were the one being interviewed, and the candidate was the one that had to be sold on Fog Creek. Which they do. Remember, the whole philosophy of recruiting is predicated on the idea that smart candidates have a choice of where to work, and if that's true, the interview process is as much a way for the candidate to decide if they want to work for us as it is a way for us to decide if we want to hire the candidate. "Do you have any questions about Fog Creek, about working at Fog Creek, or anything else you want to ask me?"

Sometimes this part of the interview reveals a frightening lack of preparation by the candidate. "So, what exactly does Fog Creek do? And where are you located?" Failing to do even the most basic homework before the interview, by spending five minutes on our website, does not give me a great deal of confidence in the candidate's ability to be smart or to get things done.

Passing a phone screen is never enough to get hired. It's nothing more than a simple filter designed to save time and expense on in-person interviews, and to eliminate candidates who will never make it before you've flown them all the way across the country and put them up in a fancy hotel. Still, even with the phone screen, probably only about one in three candidates makes it all the way through the in-person interview.

Chapter 6

THE GUERRILLA GUIDE TO INTERVIEWING

A motley gang of anarchists, free-love advocates, and banana-rights agitators have hijacked *The Love Boat* out of Puerto Vallarta and are threatening to sink it in seven days with all 616 passengers and 327 crew members unless their demands are met. The demands? A million dollars in small unmarked bills and a GPL implementation of WATFIV, that is, the esteemed Waterloo Fortran IV compiler. (It's surprising how few things the free-love people can find to agree on with the banana-rights people.)

As chief programmer of the Festival Cruise programming staff, you've got to decide if you can deliver a Fortran compiler from scratch in seven days. You've got a staff of two programmers to help you.

Can you do it?

"Well, I suppose, it depends," you say. One of the benefits of writing this book is that I get to put words into your mouth and you can't do a darn thing about it.

On what?

"Um, will my team be able to use UML-generating tools?"

Does that really matter? Three programmers, seven days, Waterloo Fortran IV. Are UML tools going to make or break it?

"I guess not."

OK, so, what does it depend on?

"Will we have 19-inch monitors? And will we have access to all the Jolt we can drink?"

Again, does this matter? Is caffeine going to determine whether you can do it?

"I guess not. Oh, wait. You said I have a staff of two programmers?"

Right.

"Who are they?"

Does that matter?

"Sure! If the team doesn't get along, we'll never be able to work together. And I know a few superstar programmers who could crank out a Fortran compiler *by themselves* in one week, and *lots* of programmers who couldn't write the code to print the startup banner if they had six months."

Now we're on to something!

Everybody gives lip service to the idea that people are the most important part of a software project, but nobody is quite sure what you can *do* about it. The very first thing you have to do right if you want to have good programmers is to *hire* the right programmers, and that means you have to be able to figure out who the right programmers *are*, and this is usually done in the interview process. So this chapter is all about interviewing.

You should always try to have at least six people interview each candidate, including at least five who would be peers of that candidate (that is, other programmers, not managers). You know the kind of company that just has some salty old manager interview each candidate, and that decision is the only one that matters? These companies don't have very good people working there. It's too easy to fake out one interview, especially when a nonprogrammer interviews a programmer.

If even two of the six interviewers thinks that a person is not worth hiring, don't hire them. That means you can technically end the "day" of interviews after the first two if the candidate is not going to be hired, which is not a bad idea, but to avoid cruelty, you may not want to tell the candidate in advance how many people will be interviewing them. I have heard of companies that allow any interviewer to reject a candidate. This strikes me as a little bit too aggressive; I would probably allow any senior person to reject a candidate but would not reject someone just because one junior person didn't like them.

Don't try to interview a bunch of people at the same time. It's just not fair. Each interview should consist of one interviewer and one interviewee, in a room with a door that closes and a whiteboard.

I can also tell you from extensive experience that if you spend less than one hour on an interview you're not going to be able to make a decision.

You're going to see three types of people in your interviews. At one end of the scale, there are the unwashed masses, lacking even the most basic skills for this job. They are easy to ferret out and eliminate, often just by asking two or three quick questions. At the other extreme, you've got your brilliant superstars who write Lisp compilers for fun, in a weekend, in Assembler for the Nintendo DS. And in the middle, you have a large number of "maybes" who seem like they might just be able to contribute something. The trick is telling the difference between the superstars and the maybes, because the secret is that you don't want to hire any of the maybes. Ever.

At the end of the interview, you must be prepared to make a sharp decision about the candidate. There are only two possible outcomes to this decision: *Hire* or *No Hire*. There is no other possible answer. *Never* say, "Hire, but not for my team." This is rude and implies that the candidate is not smart enough to work with you, but maybe he's smart enough for those losers over in that other team. If you find yourself tempted to say, "Hire, but not for my team," simply translate that mechanically to "No Hire" and you'll be OK. Even if you have a candidate who would be brilliant at doing your particular task, but wouldn't be very good in another team, that's a *No Hire*. In software, things change so often and so rapidly that you need people who can succeed at just about any programming task that you throw at them. If for some reason you find an idiot savant who is really, really, really good at SQL but completely incapable of ever learning any other topic, *No Hire*. You'll solve some short-term pain in exchange for a lot of long-term pain.

Never say, "Maybe, I can't tell." If you can't tell, that means *No Hire*. It's really easier than you'd think. Can't tell? Just say no! If you are on the fence, that means *No Hire*. Never say, "Well, Hire, I guess, but I'm a little bit concerned about ..." That's a *No Hire* as well.

Mechanically translate all the waffling to "no" and you'll be all right.

Why am I so hard-nosed about this? It's because it is much, *much* better to reject a good candidate than to accept a bad candidate. A bad candidate will cost a lot of money and effort and waste other people's time fixing all their bugs. Firing someone you hired by mistake can take months and be nightmarishly difficult, especially if they decide to be litigious about it. In some situations, it may be completely impossible to fire anyone. Bad employees demoralize the good employees. And they might be bad programmers but really *nice people* or maybe they *really need this job*, so you can't bear to fire them, or you can't fire them without pissing everybody off, or whatever. It's just a bad scene.

On the other hand, if you reject a good candidate, I mean, I *guess* in some existential sense an injustice has been done, but, hey, if they're so smart, don't worry, they'll get *lots* of good job offers. Don't be afraid that you're going to reject too many people and you won't be able to find anyone to hire. During the interview, it's not your problem. Of course, it's important to seek out good candidates. But once you're actually interviewing someone, pretend that you've got 900 more people lined up outside the door. Don't lower your standards no matter how hard it seems to find those great candidates.

OK, I didn't tell you the most important part—how do you know whether to hire someone?

In principle, it's simple. You're looking for people who are

1. Smart, and

2. Get things done.

That's it. That's all you're looking for. Memorize that. Recite it to yourself before you go to bed every night. You don't have enough time to figure out much more in a short interview, so don't waste time trying to figure out whether the candidate might be pleasant to be stuck in an airport with, or whether they really know ATL and COM programming or if they're just faking it.

People who are *Smart* but don't *Get Things Done* often have PhDs and work in big companies where nobody listens to them because they are completely impractical. They would rather mull over something academic about a problem than ship on time. These people can be identified because they love to point out the theoretical similarity between two widely divergent concepts. For example, they will say, "Spreadsheets are really just a special case of programming language," and then go off for a week and write a thrilling, brilliant whitepaper about the theoretical computational linguistic attributes of a spreadsheet as a programming language. Smart, but not useful. The other way to identify these people is that they have a tendency to show up at your office, coffee mug in hand, and try to start a long conversation about the relative merits of Java introspection vs. COM type libraries, *on the day you are trying to ship a beta.*

People who *Get Things Done* but are not *Smart* will do stupid things, seemingly without thinking about them, and somebody else will have to come clean up their mess later. This makes them net *liabilities* to the company because not only do they fail to contribute, but they soak up good people's time. They are the kind of people who decide to refactor your core algorithms to use the Visitor pattern, which they just read about the night before, and completely misunderstood, and instead of simple loops adding up items in an array you've got an `AdderVistior` class (yes, it's spelled wrong) and a `VisitationArrangingOfficer` singleton and none of your code works any more.

How do you detect *smart* in an interview? The first good sign is that you don't have to explain things over and over again. The conversation just flows. Often, the candidate says something that shows real insight, or brains, or mental acuity. So an important part of the interview is creating a situation where someone can show you how smart they are. The worst kind of interviewer is the Blowhard. That's the kind who blabs the whole time and barely leaves the candidate time to say, "Yes, that's *so* true, I *couldn't agree with you more*." Blowhards hire everyone; they think that the candidate must be smart because "he thinks so much like me!"

The second worst kind of interviewer is the Quiz Show Interviewer. This is the kind of person who thinks that smart means "knows a lot of facts." They just ask a bunch of trivia questions about programming and give points for correct answers. Just for fun, here is the worst interview question on Earth: "What's the difference between varchar and varchar2 in Oracle 8i?" This is a terrible question. There is no possible, imaginable correlation between people who know that particular piece of trivia and people whom you want to hire. Who cares what the difference is? You can find out online in about fifteen seconds! Remember, smart does *not* mean "knows the answer to trivia questions." Anyway, software teams want to hire people with *aptitude*, not a particular skill set. Any skill set that people can bring to the job will be technologically obsolete in a couple of years, anyway, so it's better to hire people who are going to be able to learn any new technology rather than people who happen to know how to make JDBC talk to a MySQL database *right this minute*.

But in general, the way to learn the most about a person is to let them do the talking. Give them open-ended questions and problems.

So, what do you ask?

My personal list of interview questions originates from my first job at Microsoft. There are actually hundreds of famous Microsoft interview questions.[1] Everybody has a set of questions that they really like. You, too, will develop a particular set of questions and a personal interviewing style that helps you make the *Hire/No Hire* decision. Here are some techniques that I have used that have been successful.

Before the interview, I read over the candidate's resume and jot down an interview plan on a scrap of paper. That's just a list of questions that I want to ask. Here's a typical plan for interviewing a programmer:

---

1. For a whole book of them, see William Poundstone, *How Would You Move Mount Fuji: Microsoft's Cult of the Puzzle* (New York: Little, Brown and Company, 2003).

1. Introduction

2. Question about recent project candidate worked on

3. Easy programming question

4. Pointer/recursion question

5. Are you satisfied?

6. Do you have any questions?

I am very, very careful to avoid anything that might give me some preconceived notions about the candidate. If you think that someone is smart before they even walk into the room, just because they have a PhD from MIT, then nothing they can say in one hour is going to overcome that initial prejudice. If you think they are a bozo because they went to community college, nothing they can say will overcome that initial impression. An interview is like a very, very delicate scale—it's very hard to judge someone based on a one-hour interview, and it may seem like a very close call. But if you know a little bit about the candidate beforehand, it's like a big weight on one side of the scale, and the interview is useless. Once, right before an interview, a recruiter came into my office. "You're going to *love* this guy," she said. *Boy* did this make me mad. What I should have said was,

"Well, if you're so sure I'm going to love him, why don't you just hire him instead of wasting my time going through this interview." But I was young and naïve, so I interviewed him. When he said not-so-smart things, I thought to myself, "Gee, must be the exception that proves the rule." I looked at everything he said through rose-colored glasses. I wound up saying *Hire* even though he was a crappy candidate. You know what? Everybody else who interviewed him said *No Hire*. So: don't listen to recruiters; don't ask around about the person before you interview them; and never, ever talk to the other interviewers about the candidate until you've both made your decisions independently. That's the scientific method.

The *introduction* phase of the interview is intended to put the candidate at ease. I ask them if they had a nice flight. I spend about thirty seconds telling the person who I am and how the interview will work. I always reassure candidates that we are interested in *how* they go about solving problems, not the actual answer.

Part two is a question about some recent project that the candidate worked on. For interviewing college kids, ask them about their senior thesis, if they had one, or about a course they took that involved a long project that they really enjoyed. For example, sometimes I will ask, "What class did you take last semester that you liked the most? It doesn't have to be computer-related." When interviewing experienced candidates, you can talk about their most recent assignment from their previous job.

Again, ask open-ended questions and sit back and listen, with only the occasional "tell me more about that" if they seem to stall.

What should you look for during the open-ended questions?

One: look for passion. Smart people are passionate about the projects they work on. They get very excited talking about the subject. They talk quickly and get animated. Being passionately *negative* can be just as good a sign. "My last boss wanted to do everything on VAX computers because it was all he understood. What a dope!" There are far too many people around who can work on something and not really care one way or the other. It's hard to get people like this motivated about anything.

Bad candidates just don't care and will not get enthusiastic at all during the interview. A really good sign that a candidate is passionate about something is that when they are talking about it, they will forget for a moment that they are in an interview. Sometimes a candidate comes in who is very nervous about being in an interview situation—this is normal, of course, and I always ignore it. But then when you get them talking about Computational Monochromatic Art, they will get extremely excited and lose all signs of nervousness. Good. I like passionate people who really care. (To see an example of Computational Monochromatic Art, try unplugging your monitor.) You can challenge them on something (try it—wait for them to say something that's probably true and say, "That couldn't be true") and they will defend themselves, even if they were sweating five minutes ago, because they care so much they forget that you are going to be making Major Decisions About Their Life soon.

Two: good candidates are careful to explain things well, at whatever level. I often reject candidates because when they talked about their previous project, they couldn't explain it in terms that a normal person could understand. Often CS majors will just assume that everyone knows what Bates Theorem is or what $O(\log n)$ means. If they start doing this, stop them for a minute and say, "Could you do me a favor, just for the sake of the exercise, could you please explain this in terms my grandmother could understand." At this point many people will *still* continue to use jargon and will completely fail to make themselves understood. *Gong!* You don't want to hire them, basically, because they are not smart enough to comprehend what it takes to make other people understand their ideas.

Three: if the project was a team project, look for signs that they took a leadership role. A candidate might say, "We were working on X, but the boss said Y, and the client said Z." I'll ask, "So what did *you* do?" A good answer to this might be "I got together with the other members of the team and wrote a proposal...." A bad answer might be, "Well, there was nothing I *could* do. It was an impossible situation." Remember, *Smart* and *Gets Things Done*. The only way you're going to be able to tell if somebody *Gets Things Done* is to see if historically they have tended to get things done in the past. In fact, you can even ask them directly to give you an example from their recent past when they took a leadership role and got something done—overcoming some institutional inertia, for example.

Most of the time in the interview, though, should be spent letting the candidate prove that they can write code.

Reassure candidates that you understand that it's hard to write code without an editor, and you will forgive them if the whiteboard gets really messy. Also you understand that it's hard to write bug-free code without a compiler, and you will take that into account.

For the first interview of the day, I've started including a really, really easy programming problem. I had to start doing this during the dotcom boom when a lot of people who thought HTML was "programming" started showing up for interviews, and I needed a way to avoid wasting too much time with them. It's the kind of problem that any programmer working today should be able to solve in about one minute. Some examples:

1. Write a function that determines if a string starts with an uppercase letter A–Z.

2. Write a function that determines the area of a circle given the radius.

3. Add up all the values in an array.

These softball questions seem too easy, so when I first started asking them, I had to admit that I really expected everyone to sail right through them. What I discovered was that everybody *solved* the problem, but there was a lot of variation in *how long* it took them to solve.

That reminded me of why I couldn't trade bonds for a living.

My partner, Jared, is a bond trader. He is always telling me about interesting deals that he did. There's this thing called an option, and there are puts, and calls, and the market steepens, so you put on steepeners, and it's all very confusing, but the weird thing is that *I know what all the words mean,* I know exactly what a put is (the right, but not the responsibility, to sell something at a certain price), and in only three minutes I can figure out what should happen if you own a put and the market goes up, but I need the *full* three minutes to figure it out, and when he's telling me a more complicated story, where the puts are just the first bit, there are lots of other bits to the story, I lose track very quickly, because I'm lost in thought ("Let's see, market goes up, that mean interest rates go *down*, and now, a put is the right to sell something ...") until he gets out the graph paper and starts walking me through it, and my eyes glazeth over and it's very sad. Even though I understand all the little bits, I can't understand them *fast enough* to get the big picture.

And the same thing happens in programming. If the basic concepts aren't so easy that you don't even have to think about them, you're not going to get the big concepts.

Serge Lang, a math professor at Yale, used to give his Calculus students a fairly simple algebra problem on the first day of classes, one which almost everyone could solve, but some of them solved it *as quickly as they could write* while others took a while, and Professor Lang claimed that all of the students who solved the problem as quickly as they could write would get an A in the Calculus course, and all the others wouldn't. The *speed* with which they solved a simple algebra problem was as good a predictor of the final grade in Calculus as a whole semester of homework, tests, midterms, and a final.[2]

You see, if you can't whiz through the *easy* stuff at 100 mph, you're never gonna get the advanced stuff.[3]

But like I said, the good programmers stand up, write the answer on the board, sometimes adding a clever fillip (Ooh! Unicode compliant! Nice!), and it takes thirty seconds, and now I have to decide if they're really good, so I bring out the big guns: recursion and pointers.

---

2. Gary Cornell, personal interview, October 27, 2006. A typical problem was to simplify $\dfrac{\dfrac{1}{x+h} - \dfrac{1}{x}}{h}$

3. Or, as Alfred North Whitehead put it, "It is a profoundly erroneous truism, repeated by all copy books and by eminent people when they are making speeches, that we should cultivate the habit of thinking of what we are doing. The precise opposite is the case. Civilization advances by extending the number of important operations which we can perform without thinking about them." From *An Introduction to Mathematics* (1911).

15 years of experience interviewing programmers has convinced me that the best programmers all have an easy aptitude for dealing with multiple levels of abstraction simultaneously. In programming, that means specifically that they have no problem with recursion (which involves holding in your head multiple levels of the call stack at the same time) or complex pointer-based algorithms (where the address of an object is sort of like an abstract representation of the object itself).

I've come to realize that understanding pointers in C is not a skill, it's an aptitude. In first-year computer science classes, there are always about 200 kids at the beginning of the semester, all of whom wrote complex adventure games in BASIC for their PCs when they were 4-years old. They are having a good ol' time learning C or Pascal in college, until one day their professor introduces pointers, and suddenly, *they don't get it*. They just don't understand anything anymore. 90% of the class goes off and becomes Political Science majors, then they tell their friends that there weren't enough good-looking members of the appropriate sex in their Comp Sci classes, that's why they switched. *For some reason most people seem to be born without the part of the brain that understands pointers*. Pointers require a complex form of doubly indirect thinking that some people just can't do, and it's pretty crucial to good programming. A lot of the "script jocks" who started programming by copying JavaScript snippets into their web pages and went on to learn Perl never learned about pointers, and they can never quite produce code of the quality you need.

That's the source of all these famous interview questions you hear about, like "reversing a linked list" or "detect loops in a tree structure."

Sadly, despite the fact that I think that all good programmers should be able to handle recursion and pointers, and that this is an excellent way to tell if someone is a good programmer, the truth is that these days, programming languages have almost completely made that specific art unnecessary. Whereas ten years ago it was rare for a computer science student to get through college without learning recursion and functional programming in one class and C or Pascal with data structures in another class, today it's possible in many otherwise reputable schools to coast by on Java alone.[4]

---

4. Joel Spolsky, "The Perils of JavaSchools," published at www.joelonsoftware.com on December 29, 2005 (search for "JavaSchools").

A lot of programmers whom you might interview these days are apt to consider recursion, pointers, and even data structures to be a silly implementation detail that has been abstracted away by today's many happy programming languages. "When was the last time you had to write a sorting algorithm?" they snicker.

Still, I don't really care. I want my ER doctor to understand anatomy, even if all she has to do is put the computerized defibrillator nodes on my chest and push the big red button, and I want programmers to know programming down to the CPU level, even if Ruby on Rails *does* read your mind and build a complete Web 2.0 social collaborative networking site for you with three clicks of the mouse.

Even though the format of the interview is, superficially, just a candidate writing some code on the whiteboard, my real goal here is to have a conversation about it. "Why did you do it that way?" "What are the performance characteristics of your algorithm?" "What did you forget?" "Where's your bug?"

That means I don't really mind giving programming problems that are too hard, as long as the candidate has some chance of starting out, and then I'm happy to dole out little hints along the way, little toeholds, so to speak.

I might ask someone, say, to project a triangle onto a plane, a typical graphics problem, and I don't mind helping them with the trig (SOH-CAH-TOA, baby!), and when I ask them how to speed it up, I might drop little hints about lookup tables. Notice that the kinds of hints I'm happy to provide are really just answers to trivia questions—the kinds of things that you find on Google.

Inevitably, you will see a bug in their function. So we come to question five from my interview plan: "Are you satisfied with that code?" You may want to ask, "OK, so where's the bug?" The quintessential Open-Ended Question From Hell. All programmers make mistakes, there's nothing wrong with that, they just have to be able to find them. With string functions in C, most college kids forget to null-terminate the new string. With almost any function, they are likely to have off-by-one errors. They will forget semicolons sometimes. Their function won't work correctly on 0 length strings, or it will GPF if malloc fails ... Very, very rarely, you will have a candidate write code that doesn't have any bugs the first time. In this case, this question is even more fun. When you say, "There's a bug in that code," they will review their code carefully, and then you get a chance to see if they're rigorous in reasoning about their code, and if they're diplomatic yet firm in asserting that the code is perfect.

As the last step in an interview, ask the candidate if they have any questions. Remember, even though you're interviewing them, the good candidates have lots of choices about where to work, and they're using this day to figure out if they want to work for you.

Some interviewees try to judge if the candidate asks "intelligent" questions. Personally, I don't care what questions they ask; by this point I've already made my decision. The trouble is, candidates have to see about five or six people in one day, and it's hard for them to ask five or six people different, brilliant questions, so if they don't have any questions, fine.

I always leave about five minutes at the end of the interview to sell the candidate on the company and the job. This is actually important *even if you are not going to hire them.* If you've been lucky enough to find a really good candidate, you want to do everything you can at this point to make sure that they want to come work for you. Even if they are a bad candidate, you want them to like your company and go away with a positive impression.

Bad Questions

Ah, I just remembered that I should give you some more examples of really bad questions.

First of all, avoid the illegal questions. Anything related to race, religion, gender, national origin, age, military service eligibility, veteran status, sexual orientation, or physical handicap is illegal here in the United States. If their resume says they were in the Marines, you can't ask them, even to make pleasant conversation, if they were in Iraq. It's against the law to discriminate based on veteran status. If their resume says that they attended the Technion in Haifa, don't ask them, even conversationally, if they are Israeli, even if you're just making conversation because your wife is Israeli, or you love falafel. It's against the law to discriminate based on national origin.

Next, avoid any questions that might make it seem like you care about, or are discriminating based on, things that you don't actually care about or discriminate based on. The best example of this I can think of is asking someone if they have kids or if they are married. This might give the impression that you think that people with kids aren't going to devote enough time to their work or that they are going to run off and take maternity leave. Basically, stick to questions that are completely relevant to the job for which they are interviewing.

Finally, avoid brain teaser questions like the one where you have to arrange six equal-length sticks to make exactly four identical perfect triangles. Or anything involving pirates, marbles, and secret codes. Most of these are "Aha!" questions—the kind of question where you either know the answer or you don't. With these questions, knowing the answer just means you heard that brain teaser before. So as an interviewer, you don't get any information about "smart/get things done" by figuring out if they happen to make a particular mental leap.

In the past, I've used "impossible questions," also known as "back of the envelope questions." A classic example of this is "How many piano tuners are there in Seattle?" The candidate won't know the answer, but smart candidates won't give up, and they'll be happy to try and estimate a reasonable number for you. Let's see, there are probably ... what, a million people in Seattle? And maybe 1% of them have pianos? And a piano needs to be tuned every couple of years? And it takes thirty-five minutes to tune one? All wrong, of course, but at least they're attacking the problem. The only reason to ask a question like this is that it lets you have a conversation with the candidate. "OK, thirty-five minutes, but what about travel time between pianos?"

"Good point. If the piano tuner could take reservations well in advance, they could probably set up their schedule to minimize travel time. You know, do all the pianos in Redmond on Monday rather than going back and forth across SR-520 three times a day."

A good back-of-the-envelope question allows you to have a conversation with the candidate that helps you form an opinion about whether they are smart. A bad "Aha!" pirate question usually results in the candidate just sort of staring at you for a while and then saying they're stuck.

If, at the end of the interview, you've convinced yourself that this person is *smart* and *gets things done*, and four or five other interviewers agree, you probably won't go wrong in hiring them. But if you have any doubts, you're better off waiting for someone better.

The optimal time to make a decision about the candidate is about three minutes after the end of the interview. Far too many companies allow interviewers to wait days or weeks before turning in their feedback. Unfortunately, the more time that passes, the less you'll remember.

I ask interviewers to write *immediate* feedback after the interview, either *Hire* or *No Hire*, followed by a one- or two-paragraph justification. It's due fifteen minutes after the interview ends.

If you're having trouble deciding, there's a very simple solution. *No Hire*. Just don't hire people that you aren't sure about. This is a little nerve wracking the first few times—what if we *never* find someone good? That's OK. If your resume and phone-screening process is working, you'll probably have about 20% hires in the live interview. And when you find the smart, gets-things-done candidate, *you'll know it*. If you're not thrilled with someone, move on.

Closing the Deal

OK. You've made a great workplace, you found the right candidates, you interviewed them well, and you're ready to make an offer. There's still time to mess up. As soon as you've identified the right person, it's time to concentrate on getting the details right so you can close the deal.

Solve Problems

Once you've made an offer, start focusing on what problems the candidate might have and get ready to spend money to solve them. Relocation? Paid for. Immigration lawyer? We'll take care of it. Can we help your spouse find a job? Need a real estate broker? Want to come visit for a house-hunting trip? We'll pay for it.

Treat Them Like Samurai

In the famous Akira Kurosawa movie *Seven Samurai*, a tiny, impoverished farming village, under constant attacks by bandits, tries to hire seven samurai to help them defend themselves. The village is poor and can barely afford to feed the samurai, let alone pay them, yet, somehow, seven virtuous samurai with mostly good hearts agree to come defend the village.

This village is your team. The samurai are the programmers who, you hope, will come solve your problems, bringing their talent and expertise in exchange for, maybe, a bowl of rice. You may be poor and hopeless, but you sure as heck know how to show some respect for the samurai who is going to save your behind.

Remember: most normal recruiting in our society is structured as if the company has something precious (a job) that the individual wants. But when you're recruiting top developers, the situation is completely reversed. Pay very, very close attention to the details of the entire recruiting, interviewing, and hiring process to make sure there are no accidental parts of the procedure that send any message other than "We're not worthy!" to your star candidates.

Coder Bob Reselman told a poignant story of going to Microsoft to interview.[5] When lunchtime came, he was left by himself in a conference room and given a box lunch. This is an absolutely reprehensible way to treat *any* guest, let alone a potential samurai who is considering coming to defend your village. Even if you've already written off someone in the morning interviews, they've gone to enormous trouble, taken off work and maybe flown across the country to volunteer to help you with your problems, and just because they're not going to be a perfect fit is no excuse to treat them with anything less than the utmost in humility and respect.

Finally, if you do have to say no to someone, do it quickly and respectfully. You are, of course, under no obligation to tell people *why* they're not the right fit, but you do have to tell them, and you have to do it promptly. It's just common decency to let them move on to the next opportunity.

---

5. On the Web at codingslave.blogspot.com/2005/03/
   q-when-is-last-time-you-behaved.html.

The Obstacle Course, Revisited

Back to the original question: how can you hire the best people? Like I said many pages ago, there's no silver bullet: there are a whole lot of problems you're going to have to solve and a lot of work you're going to have to do to reorient your company to be an attractive place for great programmers. You're going to have to focus on every single contraption on the obstacle course and work on all of them. A lot of the things you'll have to do are beyond the power of a recruiting director, hiring manager, or even the CEO, but do them you must.

In the end, you might be tempted to say, "To hell with it; I'm going to just put my damn spec up on one of those online rent-a-programmer websites and get some kid in Romania to do it for twenty bucks."

Don't give up. Great people are much, much more valuable than average people. In programming, they are three to ten times as productive, while only costing 20% or 30% more. And they hit high notes that nobody else can hit.

Chapter 7

FIXING SUBOPTIMAL TEAMS

Inheriting an existing team is sort of like being a dentist with a patient who hasn't been to see a dentist for about twenty years, and various teeth are starting to hurt. You're going to have to do three things:

1. A detailed inspection and X-ray. Figure out where the problems are: what teeth are solid; what teeth need repairs, and which teeth just need to be pulled out and replaced.

2. A lot of drilling to remove rotted areas.

3. Fillings and porcelain inlays to fill in the big gaps left by all the drilling.

It's going to be rather painful and you're going to have to put your fingers in peoples' mouths, but after a few weeks of painful work, they'll have a nice smile again. And if you're doing your sacred duty as a dentist, you will have scared them into avoiding all dentists for *another* twenty years.

I know, I know, you always tell them that they *really have to start flossing*. Let me know how *that* works out for you.

The Wrong Way to Do It: Measurement and Incentives

An extremely popular and seemingly scientific way to improve a team is with performance measurements and incentives.

For example, you might decide to start counting the lines of code that each developer generates per day. The developers with the most lines of code get a bonus. Those with average lines of code get to keep their jobs. Drop into the bottom 20% and you're fired.

This is a common management technique, and it's *devastatingly* ineffective.

The problem, of course, is that it's trivial, as a programmer, to increase the number of lines of code that you produce every day. Just put in some extra blank lines.

"Oh," you say. "Good point. We should measure *nonblank* lines of code."

"OK," say the programmers. "We'll write *lots* of comments. Long expository paragraphs with three words per line."

"Well, I appreciate the comments, but that's just cheating. I'm only going to measure *actual lines of code.*"

"OK, so, if you're not paying me to write comments, I won't write comments at all. And I'll spread out every function call so each argument is on its own line. It looks neat that way!"

"Aargh!" you think. "Maybe there's something I can measure that's harder to game. I can measure *statements*, so spreading them out on multiple lines won't change the count."

"OK. Well, I have this big block of obsolete code that I don't need any more. I really should delete it, because it's just going to confuse the heck out of the next programmer who reads the code. But if I delete 500 lines of code, it's going to make me the *worst programmer on the team* for the next two months. So I'm going to have to just wrap it in a cryptic 'if' statement so it never executes. Maybe then you won't penalize me."

We could go on and on with this dialog for a long time. Managers seem to believe that there is *some* measurement that can be used to gauge productivity, you just have to sort of tweak the rules to avoid gaming the measurement.

Programmers know that whatever you measure, they can optimize for. Trivially.

Whatever you measure.

So measurement, frankly, is hopeless.

Could it be this bad?

Yes, it turns out. Professor Robert D. Austin of Harvard Business School did a lot of research on the subject and wrote the classic of the field, *Measuring and Managing Performance in Organizations*.[1] The gist of the book is that people are not chemistry experiments, because they are self-aware, and when you try to measure things about them, they're aware of this, and they have brains they can use to get the measurement to look the way you want it to look.

He shows that whenever you institute a new metric in a knowledge organization, that is, any organization with workers who need to do something more complicated than screwing caps on toothpaste tubes, at first you see genuine improvement of the thing you want to measure. The programmers do, actually, try to write more code every day. But very soon what you see is that the workers figure out shortcuts, so the metric starts to go through the roof, while the actual performance actually declines, because

---

1. Robert D. Austin, *Measuring and Managing Performance in Organizations* (New York: Dorset House, 1996).

programmers start spending more time optimizing for metrics, which comes at the cost of the quality of work that they do.

More importantly, this is not just because you haven't figured out the perfect metric. *It's the very nature of knowledge work.*

Different Types of Contributors

Over the course of my career, I've met and worked with hundreds of talented programmers, but some of them stood out, not because they wrote great code, but because they made astonishingly valuable contributions to the organization in the ways that would never have been captured in a traditional performance review or metric.

I've known developers who are not very good at writing their own code, but are brilliant debuggers. You often find them in another developer's office because the team quickly learns to call them in for the really hard problems.

And I've known developers who seem sort of dreamy, who spend more time surfing the Internet and downloading the latest tools to try out while their code goes unwritten. Some of these developers are just plain unproductive, but some of them come up with the really big productivity ideas that improve the success of the whole organization.

I've seen a company fire a developer who was pushing an idea that would have saved the company because he wasn't getting his regular work done. I've seen a company give a terrible review to a person who single handedly kept everyone on his team happy, cheerful, and productive. All because the metrics in place just didn't have a way to recognize different types of contributors.

If it wasn't bad enough that metrics don't measure, they also screw up perfectly happy, productive teams.

True, Some Developers Just Don't Pull Their Weight

Even though metrics simply don't work with knowledge workers, it's still true that there are great developers and decent developers and crappy developers. Interestingly, everybody pretty much knows who is who. You just can't quite measure it.

You still need to triage the team into three categories:

1. Great developer

2. Needs specific improvements

3. Hopeless

If you're a new manager on a team, the fastest way to do this is by peer evaluation. You ask every member of the team to categorize every other member of the team into these three categories, with the promise of anonymity. When you see trends (everybody thinks Bob has to go), investigate.

Firing Underperformers Doesn't Always Hurt Morale

One reason many managers are terrified of getting rid of underperformers is the fear that this will reduce morale on the team.

Often, though, it has the opposite effect.

The good performers are sick of having to make up for the lame work of their coworkers.

The great developers are tired of debugging or rewriting the code that just can't possibly work. And they're frustrated that management doesn't seem to care that incompetence goes unpunished, which implies that competence goes unrewarded.

The bottom line is that cleaning house, as long as it's done all at once, can often result in improved morale.

The Rubber Room

The important thing to remember is that the poor performers are not making an *inadequate* contribution to the code. They're not just working slowly. They're making a *negative* contribution. They're actually taking time away from the good performers, who have to debug their code, fix their bugs, answer their beginner questions, and deal with the repercussions of their bad design decisions. So poor performers really need to be *off the team*.

Some organizations make it extremely difficult to fire underperformers. In the New York City school system, it's so hard to get rid of a teacher with tenure that principals don't even try. "The city payrolls include hundreds of teachers who have been deemed incompetent, violent, or guilty of sexual misconduct. Since the schools are afraid to let them teach, they put them in so-called 'rubber rooms' instead. There they read magazines, play cards, and chat, at a cost to New York taxpayers of $20 million a year," writes John Stossel in *Reason*.[2]

As a team leader, your ultimate goal is to improve the performance of the team. It would be nice if the negative performers went away, but if you can't make that happen, either because of the bureaucracy you're in, or union rules, or national laws, you're going to need a rubber room system. Anything to keep these people away from the code.

Improving Performance

Many problem developers are simply lacking the basic aptitude to be great developers. I'm pretty convinced that there is a class of people who may be very smart, but who are never going to be able to understand pointers and recursion.

---

2. John Stossel, "How to Fire an Incompetent Teacher," *Reason* (October 2006). Available on the Web at www.reason.com/news/show/36802.html.

On the other hand, a lot of developers just need specific guidance to manage their performance better. In this case, as a manager, you need to set specific, realistic, achievable goals to help them understand where to go. This is the coaching part of management.

Other teams have smart developers, but they don't quite work together in a way that results in good products. That's somewhat outside the scope of this book. But I did write another book on the topic, *Joel on Software*,[3] about all the things that software teams can do to write better code, and the principles there apply to just about any high-tech team. At the heart of that book is a concept called *The Joel Test*—twelve important things I think development teams should all be doing. A copy of *The Joel Test* appears as the appendix to this book.

---

3. Joel Spolsky, *Joel on Software: And on Diverse and Occasionally Related Matters That Will Prove of Interest to Software Developers, Designers, and Managers, and to Those Who, Whether by Good Fortune or Ill Luck, Work with Them in Some Capacity* (Berkeley, CA: Apress, 2004).

Management Methods

If you want to lead a team, a company, an army, or a country, the primary problem you face is getting everyone moving in the same direction, which is really just a polite way of saying "getting people to do what you want."

Think of it this way. As soon as your team consists of more than one person, you're going to have different people with different agendas. They want different things than you want. If you're a startup founder, you might want to make a lot of money quickly so you can retire early and spend the next couple of decades going to conferences for women bloggers. So you might spend most of your time driving around Sand Hill Road talking to VCs who might buy the company and flip it to Yahoo!. But Janice the Programmer, one of your employees, doesn't care about selling out to Yahoo!, because she's not going to make any money that way. What she cares about is writing code in the latest coolest new programming language, because it's fun to learn a new thing. Meanwhile your CFO is entirely driven by the need to get out of the same cubicle he has been sharing with the system administrator, Trekkie Monster, and so he's working up a new budget proposal that shows just how much money you would save by moving to larger office space that's two minutes from his house (what a coincidence!).

The problem of getting people to move in *your* direction (or, at least, *the same* direction) is not unique to startups, of course. It's the same fundamental problem that a political leader faces when they get elected after promising to eliminate waste, corruption, and fraud in government. The mayor wants to make sure that it's easy to get city approval of a new building project. The city building inspectors want to keep getting the bribes they have grown accustomed to.

And it's the same problem that a military leader faces. They might want a team of soldiers to charge at the enemy, even when every individual soldier would really just rather cower behind a rock and let the others do the charging.

Here are three common approaches you might take:

- The Command and Control Method
- The Econ 101 Method
- The Identity Method

You will certainly find other methods of management in the wild (there's the exotic *Devil Wears Prada* Method, the Jihad Method, the Charismatic Cult Method, and the Lurch From

One Method To Another Method). But these three are worth talking about.

The Command and Control Management Method

Frederick the Great is known for saying, "Soldiers should fear their officers more than all the dangers to which they are exposed.... Good will can never induce the common soldier to stand up to such dangers; he will only do so through fear."[4]

The Command and Control form of management is based on military management. Primarily, the idea is that people do what you tell them to do, and if they don't, you yell at them until they do, and if they still don't, you throw them in the brig for a while, and if that doesn't teach them, you put them in charge of peeling onions on a submarine, sharing two cubic feet of personal space with a lad from a farm who really never quite learned about brushing his teeth.

---

4. Frederick, King of Prussia, *Frederick the Great and the Art of War*, edited and translated by Jay Luvaas (New York: Da Capo Press, 1999).

There are a million great techniques you can use. Rent the movies *Biloxi Blues* and *An Officer and a Gentleman* for some ideas.

Some managers use this technique because they actually learned it in the military. Others grew up in authoritarian households or countries and think it's a natural way to gain compliance. Others just don't know any better. Hey, it works for the military, it should work for an Internet startup!

There are, it turns out, three drawbacks with this method in a high-tech team.

First of all, people don't really like it very much, least of all smarty-pants software developers, who are, actually, pretty smart and are used to thinking they know more than everyone else, for perfectly good reasons, because it happens to be true, and so it really, really bothers them when they're commanded to do something "because." But that's not really a good enough reason to discard this method ... we're trying to be rational here. High-tech teams have many goals, but making everyone happy is rarely goal number one.

A more practical drawback with Command and Control is that management literally does not have enough time to micromanage at this level, because there simply aren't enough managers. In the military, it's possible to give an order simultaneously to a large team of people because it's common that everyone is doing the same thing. "Clean your guns!" you can say, to a squad of 28, and then go take a brief nap and have a cool iced tea on the Officers' Club veranda. In software development teams, everybody is working on something else, so attempts to micromanage turn into *hit-and-run micromanagement*. That's where you micromanage one developer in a spurt of activity and then suddenly disappear from that developer's life for a couple of weeks while you run around micromanaging another developer. The problem with hit-and-run micromanagement is that you don't stick around long enough to see why your decisions are not working or to correct course. Effectively, all you accomplish is to knock your poor programmers off the train track every once in a while, so they spend the next week finding all their train cars and putting them back on the tracks and lining everything up again, a little bit battered from the experience.

The third drawback is that in a high-tech company the individual contributors always have more information than the "leaders," so they are really in the best position to make decisions. When the boss wanders into an office where two developers have been arguing for two hours about the best way to compress an image, the person with the *least* information is the boss, so that's the *last* person you'd want making a technical decision. I remember when Mike Maples was my great-grand-boss, in charge of Microsoft Applications; he was adamant about refusing to take sides on technical issues. Eventually, people learned that they shouldn't come to him to adjudicate. This forced people to debate the issue on the merits, and issues were always resolved in favor of the person who was better at arguing, er, I mean, issues were always resolved in the best possible way.

If Command and Control is such a bad way to run a team, why does the military use it?

This was explained to me in NCO school. I was in the Israeli paratroopers in 1986. Probably the worst paratrooper they ever had, now that I think back.

There are several standing orders for soldiers. Number one: if you are in a mine field, *freeze*. Makes sense, right? It was drilled into you repeatedly during basic training. Every once in a while, the instructor would shout out "Mine!" and everybody had to freeze just so you would get in the habit.

Standing order number two: when attacked, *run towards your attackers while shooting*. The shooting makes them take cover so they can't fire at you. Running towards them causes you to get closer to them, which makes it easier to aim at them, which makes it easier to kill them. This standing order makes a lot of sense, too.

OK, now for the Interview Question: what do you do if you're in a minefield, and people start shooting at you?

This is not such a hypothetical situation; it's a really annoying way to get caught in an ambush.

The correct answer, it turns out, is that you ignore the minefield, and run towards the attackers while shooting.

The rationale behind this is that if you freeze, they'll pick you off one at a time until you're all dead, but if you charge, only some of you will die by running over mines, so for the greater good, that's what you have to do.

The trouble is that no rational soldier would charge under such circumstances. Each individual soldier has an enormous incentive to cheat: freeze in place and let the other, more macho soldiers do the charging. It's sort of like a Prisoner's Dilemma.

In life or death situations, the military needs to make sure that they can shout orders and soldiers will obey them even if the orders are suicidal. That means soldiers need to be programmed to be obedient in a way that is not really all that important for, say, a software company.

In other words, the military uses Command and Control because it's the only way to get 18-year-olds to charge through a minefield, not because they think it's the best management method for every situation.

In particular, in software development teams where good developers can work anywhere they want, playing soldier is going to get *pretty* tedious, and you're not really going to keep anyone on your team.

The Econ 101 Management Method

Joke: A poor Jew lived in the shtetl in nineteenth-century Russia. A Cossack comes up to him on horseback.

"What are you feeding that chicken?" asks the Cossack.

"Just some bread crumbs," replies the Jew.

"How dare you feed a fine Russian chicken such lowly food!" says the Cossack, and hits the Jew with a stick.

The next day the Cossack comes back. "Now what are you feeding that chicken?" he asks the Jew.

"Well, I give him three courses. There's freshly cut grass, fine sturgeon caviar, and a small bowl of heavy cream sprinkled with imported French chocolate truffles for dessert."

"Idiot!" says the Cossack, beating the Jew with a stick. "How dare you waste good food on a lowly chicken!"

On the third day, the Cossack again asks, "What are you feeding that chicken?"

"Nothing!" pleads the Jew. "I give him a kopeck and he buys whatever he wants."

(pause for laughter)

(no?)

(ba dum dum)

(still no laughter)

(oh well)

I use the term "Econ 101" a little bit tongue-in-cheek. For my non-American readers: most US college departments have a course numbered "101," which is the basic introductory course for any field. Econ 101 management is the style used by people who know just enough economic theory to be dangerous.

The Econ 101 manager assumes that everyone is motivated by money, and that the best way to get people to do what you want them to do is to give them financial rewards and punishments to create incentives.

For example, AOL might pay their call-center people for every customer they persuade *not* to cancel their subscription.

A software company might give bonuses to programmers who create the fewest bugs.

It works about as well as giving your chickens money to buy their own food.

One big problem is that it replaces intrinsic motivation with extrinsic motivation.

Intrinsic motivation is your own, natural desire to do things well. People usually start out with a lot of intrinsic motivation. They want to do a good job. They *want* to help people understand that it's in their best interest to keep paying AOL $24 a month. They *want* to write less-buggy code.

Extrinsic motivation is a motivation that comes from outside, like when you're paid to achieve something specific.

Intrinsic motivation is much stronger than extrinsic motivation. People work much harder at things that they *actually want to do*. That's not very controversial.

But when you offer people money to do things that they wanted to do, anyway, they suffer from something called the Overjustification Effect. "I must be writing bug-free code because I like the money I get for it," they think, and the extrinsic motivation *displaces* the intrinsic motivation. Since extrinsic motivation is a much weaker effect, the net result is that you've actually *reduced* their desire to do a good job. When you stop paying the bonus, or when they decide they don't care that much about the money, they no longer think that they care about bug-free code.

Another big problem with Econ 101 management is the tendency for people to find local maxima. They'll find some way to optimize for the specific thing you're paying them, without actually achieving the thing you really want.

So for example your customer retention specialist, in his desire to earn the bonus associated with maintaining a customer, will drive the customer so crazy that the *New York Times* will run a big front-page story about how nasty your customer "service" is. Although his behavior maximizes the thing you're paying him for (customer retention), it doesn't maximize the thing you really care about (profit). And then you try to reward him for the company profit, say, by giving him 13 shares of stock, and you realize that it's not really something he controls, so it's a waste of time.

When you use Econ 101 management, you're encouraging developers to game the system.

Suppose you decide to pay a bonus to the developer with the fewest bugs. Now every time a tester tries to report a bug, it becomes a big argument, and usually the developer convinces the tester that it's not really a bug. Or the tester agrees to report the bug "informally" to the developer before writing it up in the bug tracking system. And now nobody uses the bug tracking system. The "bug count" goes way down, but the number of bugs stays the same, and you lose track of them.

Developers are clever this way. Whatever you try to measure, they'll find a way to maximize, and you'll never quite get what you want.

The biggest problem with Econ 101 management is that it's not management at all: it's *an abdication of management*. A deliberate refusal to figure out how things can be made better. It's a sign that management simply doesn't know how to teach people to do better work, so they force everybody in the system to come up with their own way of doing it.

Instead of training developers on techniques of writing reliable code, you just absolve yourself of responsibility by paying them if they do. Now every developer has to figure it out on their own.

For more mundane tasks, working the counter at Starbucks or answering phone calls at AOL, it's pretty unlikely that the average worker will figure out a better way of doing things on their own. You can go into any non-Starbucks coffee shop in the country and order a short soy caramel latte extra-hot, and you'll find that you have to keep repeating your order again and again: once to the coffee maker, again to the coffee maker when they forgot what you said, and finally to the cashier so they can figure out what to charge you. That's the result of nobody telling the workers a better way. Nobody figures it out, except Starbucks, where the standard training involves a complete system of naming, writing things on cups, and calling out orders, which ensures that customers only have to specify their drink orders once. The system, invented back at Starbucks HQ, works great, but workers at the other chains never, ever come up with it on their own.

Your customer service people spend most of the day talking to customers. They don't have the time, the inclination, or the training to figure out better ways to do things. Nobody in the customer retention crew is going to be able to keep statistics and measure which customer retention techniques work best while pissing off the fewest bloggers. They just don't care enough, they're not smart enough, they don't have enough information, and they are too busy with their real job.

As a manager, it's your job to figure out a system. That's Why You Get The Big Bucks.

If you read a little bit too much Ayn Rand as a kid, or if you took one semester of Economics, before they explained that utility is not measured in dollars, you may think that setting up simplified bonus schemes and Pay For Performance is a pretty neat way to manage. But it doesn't work. Start doing your job managing and stop feeding your chickens kopecks.

Developers, the leaves in the tree, have the most information; micromanagement or Command-and-Control barking-out of orders is likely to cause nonoptimal results. But you still have to create the system. You can't abdicate your responsibility to train your people by bribing them. Management, in general, needs to set up the system so that people can get things done, it needs to avoid displacing intrinsic motivation with extrinsic motivation, and it won't get very far using fear and barking out specific orders.

Now that I've shot down Command and Control management and Econ 101 management, there's one more method managers can use to get people moving in the right direction. I call it the Identity Method.

The Identity Management Method

The real trick to management is to make people *identify* with the goals you're trying to achieve. That's a lot trickier than the other methods, and it requires some serious interpersonal skills to pull off. But if you do it right, it works better than any other method.

The problem with Econ 101 management is that it subverts intrinsic motivation. The Identity Method is a way to *create* intrinsic motivation.

To be an Identity Method manager, you have to summon all the social skills you have to make your employees identify with the goals of the organization, so that they are highly motivated, then you need to give them the information they need to steer in the right direction.

How do you make people identify with the organization?

It helps if the organizational goals are virtuous, or perceived as virtuous, in some way. Apple creates almost fanatic identification, almost entirely through a narrative that started with a single Superbowl ad in 1984: we are against totalitarianism. Doesn't seem like a particularly bold position to take, but it worked. At my company, Fog Creek Software, we stand bravely in opposition to killing kittens. Yaaaay!

Seriously, though, a method I'm pretty comfortable with is eating together. I've always made a point of eating lunch with my coworkers, and at Fog Creek we serve catered lunches for the whole team every day and eat together at one big table. It's hard to understate what a big impact this has on making the company feel like a family, in the good way, I think. In six years, nobody has ever quit.

I'm probably going to freak out some of our summer interns by admitting this, but one of the goals of our internship program is to make people identify as New Yorkers, so they're more comfortable with the idea of moving here after college and working for us full time. We do this through a pretty exhausting list of extracurricular summer activities: two Broadway shows, a trip to the Top of the Rock, a boat ride around Manhattan, a Yankees game, an open house so they can meet more New Yorkers, and a trip to a museum; Michael and I host parties in our apartments, both as a way of welcoming the interns but also as a way for interns to visualize living in an apartment in New York, not just the dorm we stuck them in.

In general, Identity Management requires you to create a cohesive, gelled team that feels like a family, so that people have a sense of loyalty and commitment to their coworkers.

The second part, though, is to give people the information they need to steer the organization in the right direction.

Earlier today, Brett came into my office to discuss beta dates for FogBugz 6.0. He was sort of leaning towards April 2007; I was sort of leaning towards December 2006. Of course, if we started the beta in April, we would have time to do a lot more polishing and improve a lot of areas of the product; if we started it in December, we'd probably have to cut a bunch of nice new features.

What I explained to Brett, though, is that we want to hire six new people in the spring, and the chances that we'll be able to afford them without FogBugz 6.0 are much smaller. So the way I concluded the meeting with Brett was to make him understand the exact financial motivations I have for shipping earlier, and now that he knows that, I'm confident he'll make the right decision ... not necessarily *my* decision. Maybe we'll have a big upswing in sales without FogBugz 6.0, and now that Brett understands the basic financial parameters, he'll realize that maybe that means we can hold 6.0 for a few more features. The point being that by sharing information, I can get Brett to do the right thing for Fog Creek even if circumstances change. If I tried to push him around by offering him a cash reward for every day before April that he ships, his incentive would be to dump the existing buggy development build on the public *tonight*. If I tried to push him around using Command and Control management by ordering him to ship bug-free code on time, *dammit*, he might do it, but he'd hate his job and leave.

There are as many different styles of management as there are managers. I've identified three major styles, two easy, dysfunctional styles and one hard, functional style, but the truth is that many development shops manage in more of an ad-hoc, "whatever works" way that may change from day to day or person to person.

Appendix

THE JOEL TEST [1]

Have you ever heard of SEMA? It's a fairly esoteric system for measuring how good a software team is. No, *wait! Don't go off and read about SEMA!* It will take you about six years just to *understand* that stuff. So I've come up with my own, highly irresponsible, sloppy test to rate the quality of a software team. The great part about it is that it takes about three minutes. With all the time you save, you can go to medical school.

---

1. Originally published on the website *Joel on Software* (www.joelonsoftware.com) way back in 2000, *The Joel Test* has become a classic. It appears in the book *Joel on Software*, along with extensive discussion of each of the points.

    Joel Spolsky, *Joel on Software: And on Diverse and Occasionally Related Matters That Will Prove of Interest to Software Developers, Designers, and Managers, and to Those Who, Whether by Good Fortune or Ill Luck, Work with Them in Some Capacity* (Berkeley, CA: Apress, 2004).

The Joel Test

1. Do you use source control?

2. Can you make a build in one step?

3. Do you make daily builds?

4. Do you have a bug database?

5. Do you fix bugs before writing new code?

6. Do you have an up-to-date schedule?

7. Do you have a spec?

8. Do programmers have quiet working conditions?

9. Do you use the best tools money can buy?

10. Do you have testers?

11. Do new candidates write code during their interview?

12. Do you do hallway usability testing?

The neat thing about *The Joel Test* is that it's easy to get a quick **yes** or **no** to each question. You don't have to figure out lines-of-code-per-day or average-bugs-per-inflection-point. Give your team 1 point for each "yes" answer. The bummer about *The Joel Test* is that you *really shouldn't* use it to make sure that your nuclear power plant software is safe.

A score of 12 is perfect, 11 is tolerable, but 10 or lower and you've got serious problems. The truth is that most software organizations are running with a score of 2 or 3, and they need *serious* help, because companies like Microsoft run at 12 full time.

Of course, these are not the only factors that determine success or failure: in particular, if you have a great software team working on a product that nobody wants, well, people aren't going to want it. And it's possible to imagine a team of "gunslingers" that doesn't do any of this stuff that still manages to produce incredible software that changes the world. But, all else being equal, if you get these 12 things right, you'll have a disciplined team that can consistently deliver.

1. Do You Use Source Control?

I've used commercial source control packages, and I've used CVS, which is free, and let me tell you, CVS is *fine*.[2] But if you don't have source control, you're going to stress out trying to get programmers to work together. Programmers

---

2. Since I wrote this article, Subversion came out, making CVS obsolete. Subversion is even *more* fine than CVS.

have no way to know what other people did. Mistakes can't be rolled back easily. The other neat thing about source control systems is that the source code itself is checked out on every programmer's hard drive—I've never heard of a project using source control that lost a lot of code.

2. Can You Make a Build in One Step?

By this I mean: how many steps does it take to make a shipping build from the latest source snapshot? On good teams, there's a single script you can run that does a full checkout from scratch, rebuilds every line of code, makes the EXEs, in all their various versions, languages, and #ifdef combinations, creates the installation package, and creates the final media—CD-ROM layout, download website, whatever.

If the process takes any more than one step, it is prone to errors. And when you get closer to shipping, you want to have a very fast cycle of fixing the "last" bug, making the final EXEs, etc. If it takes 20 steps to compile the code, run the installation builder, etc., you're going to go crazy and you're going to make silly mistakes.

For this very reason, the last company I worked at switched from WISE to InstallShield: we *required* that the installation process be able to run, from a script, automatically, overnight, using the NT scheduler, and WISE couldn't run from the scheduler overnight, so we threw it out. (The kind folks at WISE assure me that their latest version does support nightly builds.)

3. Do You Make Daily Builds?

When you're using source control, sometimes one programmer accidentally checks in something that breaks the build. For example, they've added a new source file, and everything compiles fine on their machine, but they forgot to add the source file to the code repository. So they lock their machine and go home, oblivious and happy. But nobody else can work, so they have to go home too, unhappy.

Breaking the build is so bad (and so common) that it helps to make daily builds, to ensure that no breakage goes unnoticed. On large teams, one good way to ensure that breakages are fixed right away is to do the daily build every afternoon at, say, lunchtime. Everyone does as many checkins as possible before lunch. When they come back, the build is done. If it worked, great! Everybody checks out the latest version of the source and goes on working. If the build failed, you fix it, but everybody can keep on working with the pre-build, unbroken version of the source.

On the Excel team we had a rule that whoever broke the build, as their "punishment," was responsible for babysitting the builds until someone else broke it. This was a good incentive not to break the build, and a good way to rotate everyone through the build process so that everyone learned how it worked.

4. Do You Have a Bug Database?

I don't care what you say. If you are developing code, even on a team of one, without an organized database listing all known bugs in the code, you are going to ship low-quality code. Lots of programmers think they can hold the bug list in their heads. Nonsense. I can't remember more than two or three bugs at a time, and the next morning, or in the rush of shipping, they are forgotten. You absolutely have to keep track of bugs formally.

Bug databases can be complicated or simple. A minimal useful bug database must include the following data for every bug:

- Complete steps to reproduce the bug
- Expected behavior
- Observed (buggy) behavior
- Who it's assigned to
- Whether it has been fixed or not

If the complexity of bug tracking software is the only thing stopping you from tracking your bugs, just make a simple five-column table with these crucial fields and *start using it*.

5. Do You Fix Bugs Before Writing New Code?

The very first version of Microsoft Word for Windows was considered a "death march" project. It took forever. It kept slipping. The whole team was working ridiculous hours, the project was delayed again, and again, and again, and the stress was incredible. When the dang thing finally shipped, years late, Microsoft sent the whole team off to Cancun for a vacation, then sat down for some serious soul-searching.

What they realized was that the project managers had been so insistent on keeping to the "schedule" that programmers simply rushed through the coding process, writing extremely bad code, because the bug fixing phase was not a part of the formal schedule. There was no attempt to keep the bug count down. Quite the opposite. The story goes that one programmer, who had to write the code to calculate the height of a line of text, simply wrote "return 12;" and waited for the bug report to come in about how his function is not always correct. The schedule was merely a checklist of features waiting to be turned into bugs. In the post-mortem, this was referred to as "infinite defects methodology."

To correct the problem, Microsoft adopted something called a "zero defects methodology." Many of the programmers in the company giggled, since it sounded like management thought they could reduce the bug count by executive fiat. Actually, "zero defects" meant that at any given time, the highest priority is to eliminate bugs *before* writing any new code. Here's why.

In general, the longer you wait before fixing a bug, the costlier (in time and money) it is to fix.

For example, when you make a typo or syntax error that the compiler catches, fixing it is basically trivial.

When you have a bug in your code that you see the first time you try to run it, you will be able to fix it in no time at all, because all the code is still fresh in your mind.

If you find a bug in some code that you wrote a few days ago, it will take you a while to hunt it down, but when you reread the code you wrote, you'll remember everything and you'll be able to fix the bug in a reasonable amount of time.

But if you find a bug in code that you wrote a few *months* ago, you'll probably have forgotten a lot of things about that code, and it's much harder to fix. By that time you may be fixing somebody *else's* code, and they may be in Aruba on vacation, in which case, fixing the bug is like science: you have to be slow, methodical, and meticulous, and you can't be sure how long it will take to discover the cure.

And if you find a bug in code that has *already shipped*, you're going to incur incredible expense getting it fixed.

That's one reason to fix bugs right away: because it takes less time. There's another reason, which relates to the fact that it's easier to *predict* how long it will take to write new code than to fix an existing bug. For example, if I asked you to predict how long it would take to write the code to sort a list, you could give me a pretty good estimate. But if I asked you how to predict how long it would take to fix that bug where your code doesn't work if Internet Explorer 5.5 is installed, you can't even *guess*, because you don't know (by definition) what's *causing* the bug. It could take three days to track it down, or it could take two minutes.

What this means is that if you have a schedule with a lot of bugs remaining to be fixed, the schedule is unreliable. But if you've fixed all the *known* bugs, and all that's left is new code, then your schedule will be stunningly more accurate.

Another great thing about keeping the bug count at zero is that you can respond much faster to competition. Some programmers think of this as keeping the product *ready to ship* at all times. Then if your competitor introduces a killer new feature that is stealing your customers, you can implement just that feature and ship on the spot, without having to fix a large number of accumulated bugs.

6. Do You Have an Up-to-Date Schedule?

Which brings us to schedules. If your code is at all important to the business, there are lots of reasons why it's important to the business to know when the code is going to be done. Programmers are notoriously crabby about making schedules. "It will be done when it's done!" they scream at the business people.

Unfortunately, that just doesn't cut it. There are too many planning decisions that the business needs to make well in advance of shipping the code: demos, trade shows, advertising, etc. And the only way to do this is to have a schedule, and to keep it up to date.

The other crucial thing about having a schedule is that it forces you to decide what features you are going to do, and then it forces you to pick the least important features and *cut them* rather than slipping into featuritis (a.k.a. scope creep).

7. Do You Have a Spec?

Writing specs is like flossing: everybody agrees that it's a good thing, but nobody does it.

I'm not sure why this is, but it's probably because most programmers hate writing documents. As a result, when teams consisting solely of programmers attack a problem, they prefer to express their solution in code, rather than in documents. They would much rather dive in and write code than produce a spec first.

At the design stage, when you discover problems, you can fix them easily by editing a few lines of text. Once the code is written, the cost of fixing problems is dramatically higher, both emotionally (people hate to throw away code) and in terms of time, so there's resistance to actually fixing the problems. Software that wasn't built from a spec usually winds up badly designed and the schedule gets out of control. This seems to have been the problem at Netscape, where the first four versions grew into such a mess that management stupidly decided to throw out the code and start over. And then they made this mistake all over again with Mozilla, creating a monster that spun out of control and took *several years* to get to alpha stage.

My pet theory is that this problem can be fixed by teaching programmers to be less reluctant writers by sending them off to take an intensive course in writing. Another solution is to hire smart program managers who produce the written spec. In either case, you should enforce the simple rule "no code without spec."

8. Do Programmers Have Quiet Working Conditions?

There are extensively documented productivity gains provided by giving knowledge workers space, quiet, and privacy. The classic software management book *Peopleware*[3] documents these productivity benefits extensively.

Here's the trouble. We all know that knowledge workers work best by getting into "flow," also known as being "in the zone," where they are fully concentrated on their work and fully tuned out of their environment. They lose track of time and produce great stuff through absolute concentration. This is when they get all of their productive work done. Writers, programmers, scientists, and even basketball players will tell you about being in the zone.

The trouble is, getting into "the zone" is not easy. When you try to measure it, it looks like it takes an average of fifteen minutes to start working at maximum productivity. Sometimes, if you're tired or have already done a lot of creative work that day, you just can't get into the

---

3. Tom DeMarco and Timothy Lister, *Peopleware: Productive Projects and Teams, Second Edition* (New York: Dorset House, 1999).

zone and you spend the rest of your work day fiddling around, reading the Web, playing Tetris.

The other trouble is that it's so easy to get knocked *out* of the zone. Noise, phone calls, going out for lunch, having to drive five minutes to Starbucks for coffee, and interruptions by coworkers—*especially* interruptions by coworkers—all knock you out of the zone. If a coworker asks you a question, causing a one-minute interruption, but this knocks you out of the zone badly enough that it takes you half an hour to get productive again, your overall productivity is in serious trouble. If you're in a noisy bullpen environment like the type that caffeinated dotcoms love to create, with marketing guys screaming on the phone next to programmers, your productivity will plunge as knowledge workers get interrupted time after time and never get into the zone.

With programmers, it's especially hard. Productivity depends on being able to juggle a lot of little details in short-term memory all at once. Any kind of interruption can cause these details to come crashing down. When you resume work, you can't remember any of the details (like local variable names you were using, or where you were up to in implementing that search algorithm) and you have to keep looking these things up, which slows you down a lot until you get back up to speed.

Here's the simple algebra. Let's say (as the evidence seems to suggest) that if we interrupt a programmer, even for a minute, we're really blowing away fifteen minutes of productivity. For this example, let's put two programmers, Jeff and Mutt, in open cubicles next to each other in a standard Dilbert veal-fattening farm. Mutt can't remember the name of the Unicode version of the `strcpy` function. He could look it up, which takes thirty seconds, or he could ask Jeff, which takes fifteen seconds. Since he's sitting right next to Jeff, he asks Jeff. Jeff gets distracted and loses fifteen minutes of productivity (to save Mutt fifteen seconds).

Now let's move them into separate offices with walls and doors. Now when Mutt can't remember the name of that function, he could look it up, which still takes thirty seconds, or he could ask Jeff, which now takes forty-five seconds and involves standing up (not an easy task given the average physical fitness of programmers!). So he looks it up. So now Mutt loses thirty seconds of productivity, but we save fifteen minutes for Jeff. Ahhh!

9. Do You Use the Best Tools Money Can Buy?

Compiling code is one of the last things that still can't be done instantly on a garden variety home computer. If your compilation process takes more than a few seconds, getting the latest and greatest computer is going to save you time. If compiling takes even fifteen seconds, programmers will get bored while the compiler runs and switch over to reading *The Onion*, which will suck them in and kill hours of productivity.

Debugging GUI code with a single monitor system is painful if not impossible. If you're writing GUI code, two monitors will make things much easier.

Most programmers eventually have to manipulate bitmaps for icons or toolbars, and most programmers don't have a good bitmap editor available. Trying to use Microsoft Paint to manipulate bitmaps is a joke, but that's what most programmers have to do.

At my last job, the system administrator kept sending me automated spam complaining that I was using more than—get this—220 megabytes of hard drive space on the server. I pointed out that given the price of hard drives these days, the cost of this space was significantly less than the cost of the *toilet paper* I used. Spending even ten minutes cleaning up my directory would be a fabulous waste of productivity.

Top-notch development teams don't torture their programmers. Even minor frustrations caused by using underpowered tools add up, making programmers grumpy and unhappy. And a grumpy programmer is an unproductive programmer.

To add to all this ... programmers are easily bribed by giving them the coolest, latest stuff. This is a far cheaper way to get them to work for you than actually paying competitive salaries!

10. Do You Have Testers?

If your team doesn't have dedicated testers, at least one for every two or three programmers, you are either shipping buggy products, or you're wasting money by having $100/hour programmers do work that can be done by $30/hour testers. Skimping on testers is such an outrageous false economy that I'm simply blown away that more people don't recognize it.

11. Do New Candidates Write Code During Their Interview?

Would you hire a magician without asking them to show you some magic tricks? Of course not.

Would you hire a caterer for your wedding without tasting their food? I doubt it. (Unless it's Aunt Marge, and she would hate you for*ever* if you didn't let her make her "famous" chopped liver cake.)

Yet, every day, programmers are hired on the basis of an impressive resume or because the interviewer enjoyed chatting with them. Or they are asked trivia questions ("What's the difference between CreateDialog() and DialogBox()?") that could be answered by looking at the documentation. You don't care if they have memorized thousands of trivia about programming, you care if they are able to produce code. Or, even worse, they are asked "AHA!" questions: the kind of questions that seem easy when you know the answer, but if you don't know the answer, they are impossible.

Please, just *stop doing this*. Do whatever you want during interviews, but make the candidate *write some code*.

12. Do You Do Hallway Usability Testing?

A *hallway usability test* is where you grab the next person that passes by in the hallway and force them to try to use the code you just wrote. If you do this to five people, you will learn 95% of what there is to learn about usability problems in your code.

Good user interface design is not as hard as you would think, and it's crucial if you want customers to love and buy your product.

But the most important thing about user interfaces is that if you show your program to a handful of people (in fact, five or six is enough), you will quickly discover the biggest problems people are having. Even if your UI design skills are lacking, as long as you force yourself to do hallway usability tests, which cost nothing, your UI will be much, much better.

INDEX